The Occult Roots of Postgenderism

And a History of Changes to Psychiatry and Psychology

by Ken Ammi

The tradition that mankind was anciently hermaphrodite is world-old
—Magus Incognito

No End Books

"…of making many books there is no end;
and much study is a weariness of the flesh.
Let us hear the conclusion of the whole matter:
Fear God, and keep his commandments:
for this is the whole duty of man."
—Ecclesiastes 12

Copyright © 2017 AD
Ken Ammi
truefreethinker.com
Cover by Ken Ammi using William Blake's painting, "Sata Amor Adao Eva" which is public domain in the United States because it was published (or registered with the U.S. Copyright Office) before January 1, 1923 AD.

Introduction

> *The tradition that mankind was anciently hermaphrodite is world-old*
> —Magus Incognito

If you have not heard about the *postgender* movement then welcome to yet another movement that is fundamentally changing our culture from behind the scenes. This movement is making inroads via politics, technology, societal activism, etc.

The "sexual revolution" was, in reality, sexual devolution and "free sex" resulted in slavery to sex.
The free sex revolution was merely an open door to homosexuality.
In turn, homosexuality was merely an open door to transgenderism.
Finally, transgenderism was merely an open door to postgenderism.

By *postgenderism* I am not referring to transitioning from one gender into the other. In fact, LGBTQIAP+ activists have already complained that the only options of transitional from *one* gender into *the* other is to restrict them into a societally fabricated gender binary and that they, particularly with the high tech de jour, can choose to be both or neither—or, perhaps neo-genders of their own invention.

Thus, the term *postgender* is being employed as literally *post* as in after and as we are told that *gender* is not biological but a mental/societal construct, it becomes that which one wills. Likewise with *transgender* wherein *trans* can refer to transitioning as well as transforming and transcending. Thus, androgyny and hermaphroditism are forms of this concept of *trans*.

We have attempted to deconstruct logic, deconstruct ethics and, in short, to deconstruct truth itself, reality itself. We are now at the point where we are seeking to deconstruct ourselves. An outworking of ultimate rebellion is to seek to deconstruct God's design for marriage and gender so as to deny that we are made in God's image. Thus, we seek to reinvent ourselves in our own image.

As of recent history, to *LGBT* was added a *Q* and then the *IA* to which I added the *P* and to which personages within that movement added the + thus, LGBTQIAP+.
Here are the meanings:
L: lesbian. G: gay. B: bisexual. T: transgendered or transsexual. Q: queer. I: intersex. A: asexual. P: postgender. +: miscellaneous.

I will employ the term *occult*, which merely means *hidden*, as a generic reference to that which could include magick, mysticism, alchemy (and mystical alchemy), witchcraft, etc.

Virtually any and every occult secret society mystery religion maintains that the concept of *god* and/or the perfect human as being an androgynous or hermaphroditic being is *hidden* knowledge that is literally becoming mainstream with, as recent news as an example, a mere eight year old deciding to pick their very own gender expression and the parents going right along with it (actually, the more likely case is that the parents manipulated the child as normal eight-year-olds come to no such conclusions if they could even be imagined to ponder such issues).

Occultism claims that the creator God, YHVH the God of the Bible, is an oppressive God who wanted to keep humanity nice and ignorant-like. Conversely, they claim that Satan (the serpent) is humanity's savior who brought us enlightenment by encouraging Eve to eat from the Tree of Knowledge (the TV show *Ancient Aliens* series made this exact point[1]). Of course, the Tree is that of the Knowledge of Good and Evil. Now, since good is referenced numerous times within Genesis prior to the eating of the forbidden fruit what, pray tell, could have been accomplished by eating therefrom but the gaining of evil?

Some proponents of the view that humanity was originally androgynous or hermaphroditic claim that the Bible states or implies as much in stating that God made, both, males and females in His image. This is something considered specifically within chapter Manly P. Hall *"man was primarily androgynous."*

Moreover, such misinterpretations of the Bible are late dated such as:
Samuel ben/bar Nahman/Nahmani: early 3rd c. early 4th c. AD.
The 5th century AD *Midrash Bereshith Rabbah* has Rabbi Yeremiah claiming that Adam was created an androgynous and Rabbi Sh'muel bar Nachman following up with that Adam had two faces and that the LORD "sawed him asunder, and split him (in two), making one back to the one-half, and another to the other."

Rabbi Moshe ben Maimon aka Rambam aka Maimonides: 1135-1204 AD.

Rabbi Manoel Dias Soeiro aka Menasseh ben Israel aka Menasheh ben Yossef ben Yisrael: 1604-1657 AD.

That which follows is that which it is: a survey of literature which touched upon such topics. Thus, this is not about individuals who face the difficult and complex issue of feeling as if they do not fit their own bodies: people with whom we must empathize. Rather, this is about the bigger picture and movement which drives it.

Table of Contents

Introduction 1
Table of Contents 5
A Succinct Sampling 7
Various Historical and Occult References 9
Hargrave Jennings' "The Rosicrucians, Their Rites and Mysteries" 17
Hermaphrodite in the Royal Museum's Cabinet Secret 25
Helena Petrovna Blavatsky's Theosophy 31
    Postgenderism Symbolism 31
    Root Races 41
    "Jesus clad in woman's clothes" 48
    Darwinian Evolution 51
The Apocryphal Ophiolatreia 57
Matilda Joslyn Gage on Matriarchy, Mound Builders and the Bible 61
W. Scott-Elliot's "The Lost Lemuria" 69
John M. Robertson on Double-Sexed Pagan Deities 73
Edward Carpenter "Intermediate Types Among Primitive Folk" 77
Donald A. Mackenzie's "Myths of Crete and Pre-Hellenic Europe" 87
Magus Incognito's "The Secret Doctrine of the Rosicrucians" 89
Ernest Holmes' New Thought Religious Science 93
Manly P. Hall "man was primarily androgynous" 95
The Androgynous Zodiac 103
The Hawaiian Creation Chant Kumulipo 105

The Book of Shadows 109
Postgenderism: Beyond the Gender Binary 111
    Postgenderism as Transhumanist Technology 115
    The "Feminist Revolution" and Postgenderism 121
    The Postgenderism Re-Education of Culture 125
    The Postgenderism Worldview and Literature 129
Intro to the Appendices 133
Appendix: Dr. Phil McGraw 137
Appendix: History of Homosexual Socio-Political Psychiatric Activism 141
    Speculative Causes of Homosexuality 162
    Is Homosexuality a Choice? 163
    Children Issues 164
    To Remove or Not to Remove? Insurance is the Question 165
    Same-Sex Marriage 167
Appendix: Dr. Kenneth Zucker and "Transgender Kids: Who Knows Best?" 169
    Discredited by Science or LGBTQIAP+ Activism? 170
    Therapy Based on Science or LGBTQIAP+ Activism? 173
    "Transgender Kids: Who Knows Best?" Documentary Could Lead to LGBTQP Suicides 178
Appendix: Is LGBTQIAP+ Parenting Good for Children? 183
Appendix: Edgar Cayce, Six-fingered Giants and the Supernatural Creation Gods of Atlantis" 189
Index 205
Endnotes 211

A Succinct Sampling

So as to immediately emphasize and evidence the assertion of occult roots of transgenderism here is a sample of that which will follow within this text.

According to occultism, by any other name, the ultimate conception of God and therefore humanity is a monad, a perfect unity.

Thus, the male and female distinction is viewed as disunity with the ultimate spiritual evolution being a combination of the two, the gender binary, into that which is claimed to have been the original perfection: one unified gender.

"The tradition that mankind was anciently hermaphrodite is world-old"
—Magus Incognito, *The Secret Doctrine of the Rosicrucians* (1918 AD).

"That man was primarily androgynous is quite universally conceded and it is a reasonable presumption that he will ultimately regain this bi-sexual state"
—Manly P. Hall, *The Secret Teachings of All Ages* (1928 AD)

"It is evident that the conception of a double sex, or of a sex combining the characters of male and female, haunted the minds of early peoples"
—Edward Carpenter, *Intermediate Types among Primitive Folk* (1914 AD)

"…the mythology of the Ancients…recognizes…the nature of Male and Female…in mystic union…constitute the

Great Hermaphrodite Deity…the Pantheons of the ancient nations…acknowledged the same deities"
—Isaac P. Cory, *Ancient Fragments* (1923 AD)

"In almost every primitive mythology we find, not only a Great Father and Mother, the representatives of the reciprocal principles, and a Great Hermaphrodite Unity from whom the first proceed and in whom they are both combined"
—the anonymously authored *Ophiolatreia* (1889 AD)

"Seeing the generative process in the union of the sex organs, primitive man came to conceive of it as essentially hermaphroditic in nature"
—B.Z. Goldberg, *The Sacred Fire* (1930 AD)

"Amaury de Chartres…held…that at the end of the world—both sexes should be re-united in the same person"
—Hargrave Jennings, *The Rosicrucians - Their Rites and Mysteries* (1870 AD)

Various Historical and Occult References

Having gotten a succinct sampling, we now dig a little deeper.

Isaac P. Cory, *Ancient Fragments* (1923 AD, intro. 34):
> By comparing all the varied legends of the East and West in conjunction we obtain the following outline of the mythology of the Ancients: It recognises, as the primary elements of things, two independent principles of the nature of Male and Female; and these, in mystic union, as the soul and body, constitute the Great **Hermaphrodite** Deity, THE ONE, the universe itself, consisting still of the two separate elements of its composition, modified though combined in one individual, of which all things are regarded but as parts......
> If we investigate the Pantheons of the ancient nations, we shall find that each, notwithstanding the variety of names, acknowledged the same deities and the same system of theology; and, however humble any of the deities may appear, each who has any claim to antiquity will be found ultimately, if not immediately, resolvable into one or other of the Primeval Principles, the Great God and Goddess of the Gentiles [ellipses in original].

The text *The Divine Pymander - Hermes Mercurius Trismegistus* (1650 AD) is attributed to Hermes. In the section "The Second Book, Called, Poemander" it states:
> And from this cause *Man*…being above all *Harmony*, he is made and become a servant to *Harmony*, he is **Hermaphrodite**, or Male and Female, and watchful, he is governed by and subjected to a Father, that is both Male and Female, and watchful.

C.A. Musés notes the following in *Esoteric Teachings of the Tibetan Tantra* (1961 AD), Part I, "Seven Initiation Rituals of the Tibetan Tantra," chap. I, "The Initiation Ritual of the Fierce Guru":
> With fiery anger he wrenched out the hearts of all the Eight-Divisional Demons, and crushed them on the plain. Afterward he revived them and said:
>> "When hungry I am the being who eats the flesh of the male demons. When thirsty, I drink the blood of the she-demons. When active, I tear the **double-sexed** demons to pieces."

B.Z. Goldberg noted the following in *The Sacred Fire* (1930 AD), chap. I, p. 202, "Love in the Synagogue":
> Just as the universe is a dualism seeking unity, so was man himself originally dual; for God created man two-faced, that is **double-sexed**, and cut him asunder into male and female. Ever since that separation was accomplished, neither man nor woman has been complete alone. To realize one's self, to find completion and harmony, he must seek union with his mate of the opposite sex.

In chap. III, "In the Foundry of the Gods" he notes:
>Here again the evolution of the generative god followed the development of sex in nature. As man came to clothe his sex god with the human form, he had one individual contain **both sex organs**. Janus of the Greeks was not only double-headed, but also **double-sexed, hermaphroditic**, like a plant that produces both stamens and pistils in the same floral envelope. Siva, the great god of India, is the Reproducer. He was originally a single substance; but of his own free will he divided himself into male and female.

On p. 96, chap. V, "Love's Hidden Ways" Goldberg wrote:
>Seeing the generative process in the union of the sex organs, primitive man came to conceive of it as essentially **hermaphroditic** in nature. And so the scarab, because it was believed to be **double-sexed** and capable of fructifying itself, became a sacred emblem. It was symbolic of the generative force in nature.
>In Egypt, it was the emblem of Khefera, god of creation, father of gods and men, creator of all things and the rising sun. In times of famine and poverty in medieval Europe, the people resorted to an old symbolic service to secure divine aid.
>In some places, the "need-fire" was kindled by two naked men, who rubbed two dry sticks together, an action in itself symbolic of the sexual process. With the flame they lighted two fires between which the cattle were driven to ensure fertility in the herd. In

other places the monks kindled the fire in the presence of the faithful. Near the fire they raised the image of the lingam.

The anonymous author of *The Hermetic Arcanum - The Secret Work of the Hermetic Philosophy* who is said to elucidate, "the secrets of nature and art concerning the matter of the philosophers' stone and the manner of working are explained in an authentic and orderly manner" wrote:

> 46. The Philosophers' Mercury hath divers names, sometimes it is called Earth; sometimes Water, when viewed from a diverse aspect; because it naturally ariseth from them both. The earth is subtle, white and sulphurous, in which the elements are fixed and the philosophical gold is sown; the water is the water of life, burning, permanent, most clear, called the water of gold and silver; but this Mercury, because it hath in it Sulphur of its own, which is multiplied by art, deserves to be called the Sulphur of Argent vive. Last of all, the most precious substance is Venus, the ancient **Hermaphrodite, glorious in its double sex**
> ...
> 58. Recipe then the Winged Virgin very well washed and cleansed, impregnated by the spiritual seed of the first male, and fecundated in the permanent glory of her untouched virginity, she will be discovered by her cheeks dyed with a blushing colour; join her to the second, by whose seed she shall conceive again and shall in time bring forth a reverend off-spring of **double sex**,

from whence an immortal Race of most potent Kings shall gloriously arise.

Ante-Nicene Fathers, Vol. VIII, chap. XVII, "Gentile Cosmogony":

> And I immediately rejoined: "Seeing that when you were disputing at Tripolis, as I said, you discoursed much concerning the gods of the Gentiles profitably and convincingly, I desire to set forth in your presence the ridiculous legends concerning their origin, both that you may not be unacquainted with the falsehood of this vain superstition, and that the hearers who are present may know the disgraceful character of their error.
>
> The wise men, then, who are among the Gentiles, say that first of all things was chaos; that this, through a long time solidifying its outer parts, made bounds to itself and a sort of foundation, being gathered, as it were, into the manner and form of a huge egg, within which, in the course of a long time, as within the shell of the egg, there was cherished and vivified a certain animal; and that afterwards, that huge globe being broken, there came forth a certain kind of man of **double sex**, which they call **masculo-feminine**.
>
> This they called Phanetas, from appearing, because when it appeared, they say, then also light shone forth. And from this, they say that there were produced substance, prudence, motion, and coition, and from these the heavens and the earth were made. From the heaven they say that six males

were produced, whom they call Titans; and in like manner, from the earth six females, whom they called Titanides.
And these are the names of the males who sprang from the heaven: Oceanus, Cœus, Crios, Hyperion, Iapetus, Chronos, who amongst us is called Saturn. In like manner, the names of the females who sprang from the earth are these: Theia, Rhea, Themis, Mnemosyne, Tethys, Hebe.

Ovid's *Metamorphoses* (1717 AD) includes the following statement within "Book the Fourth":
So pray'd the nymph, nor did she pray in vain:
For now she finds him, as his limbs she prest,
Grow nearer still, and nearer to her breast;
'Till, piercing each the other's flesh, they run
Together, and incorporate in one:
Last in one face are both their faces join'd,
As when the stock and grafted twig combin'd
Shoot up the same, and wear a common rind:
Both bodies in a single body mix,
A single body with a double sex.

Albert Pike wrote the following in *Morals and Dogma of the Ancient and Accepted Scottish Rite of Freemasonry* (1871 AD), XXVIII, "Knight of the Sun, or Prince Adept":
The doctrine of Ocellus was the general doctrine everywhere, it naturally occurring to all to make the same distinction. The Egyptians did so, in selecting those animals in which they recognized these emblematic

qualities, in order to symbolize the **double sex** of the Universe.

Their God KNEPH, out of whose mouth issued the Orphic egg, whence the author of the Clementine Recognitions makes a **hermaphroditic** figure to emerge, uniting in itself the two principles whereof Heaven and the earth are forms, and which enter into the organization of all beings which the heavens and the earth engender by their concourse, furnishes another emblem of the double power, active and passive, which the ancients saw in the Universe, and which they symbolized by the egg.

Orpheus, who studied in Egypt, borrowed from the theologians of that country the mysterious forms under which the science of nature was veiled, and carried into Greece the symbolic egg, with its division into two parts or causes figured by the **hermaphroditic** being that issued from it, and whereof Heaven and earth are composed.

Eliphas Levi's illustration Baphomet combines female features such as breasts with male features such as a phallus stylized as a caduceus.
Note the terms *solve* and *coagula* upon the arms: these refer to alchemical/chemistry in terms of *solution* and *dissolution*.

Hargrave Jennings' "The Rosicrucians, Their Rites and Mysteries"

With this chapter, we move into consuming larger swaths of literature ranging a time span from 1870 AD to 2008 AD to which I comment along the way.

The following is noted within chap. 11 "The Pre-Adamites. Profound Cabalistic or Rosicrucian Speculations" of Hargrave Jennings' *The Rosicrucians - Their Rites and Mysteries* (1870 AD):

> The "Sexes" were "Two". But "Beauty" was "One". Beards have naught of beauty, apart from strength. Beards are barbarous—hence their name. Hair is of the beasts, "*excrementa*"; "*tentacula*". The Greek artists exercised their talents in the production of a kind of beauty mixed of that of the "Two Sexes", merging and blending the softness and enchanting shapeliness of the one with the aggressive picturesque roundness and boldness of the other.
>
> Each (separate) was the acmé of picture like propriety and grace. But the third "Thing" was a "New Thing"—otherwise a miracle—a new sensation. Hence Paris, hence Adonis, hence Ganymede, hence the loves of Salmacis and **Hermaphroditus**, hence the "feminine" Bacchus, hence Hylas—hence

these deities, in tresses, of neither sex, and yet of both. Greek art in this respect presents a phenomenon. As a phenomenon we must recognize and regard it.

The flower is *supra-natural*, treasonous, and abhorrent. It is "a flower of Hell". Nevertheless, it is a "flower". And thus the idea dominates the *alternate "shaded" and "shining" halves* of the whole world; of all art; of all philosophy; of all RELIGION...

The most difficult problem of the Greek artists was to exercise their talent in the production of a kind of beauty mixed with that of the Two Sexes, and time has spared some of the masterpieces. Such is the figure known under the name of the **Hermaphrodite** (*Hermes-Aprodite; Venus-Mercury*). In the classic times, both amongst the Greeks and Romans, as also in Oriental countries, a cruel and flagitious *violation* of nature (not supposed-so; even accepted as sacred) produced this beauty by enforcing sacrifice of a peculiar kind on young male victims.

In the case of true **Hermaphroditism**, that which art could only effect by dispossession, nature brings about by super-addition, or rather by concurrent transformation or mutual "coincidence". The idea even lies "*perdue*" (like a silver snake) in the supposed origin of "Mankind." The most extraordinary ideas as to the origin of the human race have been entertained by speculative thinkers, and by theologians. The celebrated William Law believed that the First Human Being was a creature combining the characteristics of both sexes in his own individual person.

"God created man in His own Image. In the Image of God created He him." Some controversionists consider that there is a LONG space due (but not allowed) between the foregoing and the succeeding: "Male and Female created He THEM"...

We are now into territory upon which I comment within chapter *Manly P. Hall "man was primarily androgynous"* so please see that chapter for details.

Hargrave Jennings further comments thusly along these lines:

> The idea that Adam and Eve were both originally **Hermaphrodites** was revived in the thirteenth century by Amaury de Chartres. He held—among other fanciful notions—that at the end of the world—both sexes *should be re-united in the same person.*
>
> Some learned Rabbis asserted that Adam was created *double*; that is, with two bodies, one *male* and the other *female*, joined together by the shoulders; their heads (like those of Janus) looking in opposite directions. And that, when God created Eve, He only *divided* such body in Two. Others maintained that Adam and Eve were each of them, separately, an **Hermaphrodite**.

> Other Jewish authorities, among whom are Samuel Manasseh and Ben-Israel, are of opinion that our Great Progenitor was created with Two Bodies, and that "HE" separated them afterwards during Adam's sleep; an opinion founded by these writers upon the second chapter of Genesis, verse 21: 'the literal translation of the Hebrew being: "He (God) separated the Woman from his side, and substituted Flesh in her place."

Note that Manoel Dias Soeiro aka Menasseh ben Israel aka Menasheh ben Yossef ben Yisrael lived 1604-1657 AD. *Other Jewish authorities* who also engaged in such fanciful and mystical reinterpretations are also late dated in relation to when Genesis was written such as Samuel ben/bar Nahman/Nahmani who lived early 3rd c. early 4th c. AD and Rabbi Moshe ben Maimon aka Maimonides and aka RaMBaM lived 1135-1204 AD.

Jennings also notes:
> This idea resembles that of Plato. Origen, St. Chrysostom, and St. Thomas believed that the Woman was not created till the Seventh Day. But the most generally received opinion is, that Adam and Eve were created on the *Sixth*. These particular notions—extravagant as they must be admitted to be—as to the original "single-dual, dual-single" characteristics of Adam and Eve are eminently Platonic—nay, cabalistic [Kabbalistic]...

Shakespeare has several covert allusions to the dignity of the myth of the "Horns". There is much more, probably, in these spoils of the chase—the branching horns or the antlers—than is usually supposed. They indicate infinitely greater things than when they are only seen placed aloft as sylvan trophies.

The crest of his late Royal Highness Prince Albert displays the Runic horns, or the horns of the Northern mythic hero. They were always a mark of princely and of conquering eminence, and they are frequently observable in the crests and blazon of the soldier-chiefs, the Princes of Germany. They come from the original Taut, Tat, Thoth, Teat, whence "Teuton" and "Teutonic".

These names derive from the mystic Mercurius Trismegistus, "Thrice-Master; Thrice Mistress"—for this personage is **double-sexed**: "Phoebe above, Diana on earth, Hecate below."

Under the pseudonym *Sha Rocco,* Jennings wrote the following in *The Masculine Cross and Ancient Sex Worship* (1874 AD), III, Unity:
>MANY are the efforts made to set forth to the eye the conception of Deity in one person.
>The idea has evidently been one of growth from the crude to the more acceptable; and the result attained denotes composite labor. Fig. 12 is a figure of this kind.

It is a copy of an original drawing made by a learned Hindu pundit, for Wm. Simpson, Esq., of London.

It represents Brahma Supreme, who, in the act of creation, made himself **double, i.e., male and female**, as indicated by the *crux ansata* in the central part of the figure, which occupies the place of the conjoined triad and yoni of the original; the original being far too grossly shown for the public eye.

The reader will notice the triad formed by the thumb and two fingers and serpent in the male hand, while in the female hand is to be seen a germinating seed, indicative of reproduction of **father and mother**. The

whole stands upon a lotus flower, the
symbol of **androgenity**.

FYI: *crux ansata* is an aka for the Egyptian *ankh* which is a symbol that means *life*.

The Occult Roots of Postgenderism

Male and female combination along with male solar and female lunar symbolism.

Hermaphrodite in the Royal Museum's Cabinet Secret

Colonel Stanislas Marie César Famin (1799-1853 AD) made some interesting comments with regards to ancient works of art depicting hermaphrodites in *The Royal Museum at Naples, Being Some Account of the Erotic Paintings, Bronzes, and Statues Contained in that Famous "Cabinet Secret"* (1871 AD).

An Hermaphrodite and Faun. Painting Found at Resina. Plate XLI is commented upon thusly:

This painting is evidently allegorical. The old Silenus, seated on a rock, and seeking to enjoy a being who unites in himself the two senses, is the emblem of those old men, given up to debauchery, who endeavour to reanimate their deadened passions by excess and variety of enjoyment.

The taste of some old men for both sexes is a consequence of the impotency of their resources; they would fain rekindle, by the refinement and monstrosity of their pleasures, a spark of the sacred fire which animates Youth. Such, we think, was the idea which guided the capricious pencil of the author of this fresco.

Plate XL.

An Hermaphrodite. Plate XL is commented upon thusly:

THIS figure represents an hermaphrodite full of grace, youth, and beauty...The hermaphrodite here represented gracefully raises the mantle in which he is enveloped, and reveals at one and the same time the organ of virility and a woman's breast. An attentive examination of this painting will show that such a being could not exist. The beauty which glows in every one of his limbs; the softness revealed by the rounded forms; everything, in this figure, betrays a sensible and passive being, created for resistance and defeat; there is nothing there, on the other hand, to indicate the vigour and boldness of character which is the birthright of the sex made to attack and to conquer.

A Satyr and Hermaphrodite. Fresco from Pompeii. Plate XLII is commented upon thusly:

A SATYR has surprised a nymph asleep in a solitary place. He prepares to violate her, and already having lifted up the veil that envelops her, he casts a profane look on her most secret charms; but imagine his confusion on perceiving that he has accosted a hermaphrodite!

Full of shame and vexation, he seeks to fly; but the hermaphrodite, whose sleep was doubtless only a feint, tries to hold him, and seems himself to promise him pleasures of which he had not dreamt.

In order that nothing may be wanting to complete the obscenity of this painting, we observe in the background a Hermes, crowned with the petasus, bearing in one hand the pedum, or pastoral crook, and in the other the drinking-vessel, in the shape of a horn, called κρατὴρ.

As we have already remarked, these Hermes, with gigantic phalluses, were placed at the entrance of gardens to keep away robbers and sorcerers. They generally bore an inscription the idea of which was as pleasant as the expression was unseemly. We will quote two, taken at random from the collection entitled Priapeia:
> Fœmina [Femina] si furtum faciet
> mihi virque puerque, Hæc cunnum,
> caput hic, præbeat ille nates.

The Latin quote is from "Priapeia: sive diversorum poetarum in Priapum lusus" meaning, "Sportive Epigrams on Priapus by divers poets in English verse and prose" (trans by Leonard C. Smithers and Sir Richard Burton, 1890 AD). Priapus 21 translated the Latin as:

> An fro' me woman shall thieve or plunder
> me man or a man-child, she shall pay me
> with coynte, that with his mouth, this with
> arse.
> If a woman, man, or boy, thieve from me, let
> her coynte, his mouth, the latter's buttocks,
> be submitted [to my mentule].

The second, above referenced quote is from Priapus 5:

> Quod sim ligneus, ut vides, Priapus, et falx
> lignea, ligneusque penis: prendam te tamen
> et tenebo prensam: totamque hanc sine
> fraude, quantacumque est, Tormento,
> citharaque tensiorem, ad costam tibi
> septimam recondam.
>
> Though I be wooden Priapus (as thou see'st),
> with wooden sickle and a prickle of wood,
> yet will I seize thee, girl! And hold thee
> seized and This, however gross, withouten
> fraud sStiffer than lyre-string or than twisted
> rope I'll thrust and bury to thy seventh rib.

Such is the perversity of Pagan cultures.

Helena Petrovna Blavatsky's Theosophy

Postgenderism Symbolism

Helena Petrovna (H.P.) Blavatsky also noted the following in her book *The Secret Doctrine*, Vol. 2, Stanza I, "Beginnings of Sentient Life":

>...every Race in its evolution is said to be born under the direct influence of one of the Planets: Race the first receiving its breath of life from the Sun, as will be seen later on; while the third humanity — those who fell into generation, or from **androgynes** became separate entities, one male and the other female — are said to be under the direct influence of Venus, "the little sun in which the solar orb stores his light..."
>
>*"It is through Sukra that the 'double ones' (the **Hermaphrodites**) of the Third (Root-Race) descended from the first 'Sweat-born,'" says the Commentary. Therefore it is represented under the symbol of [see image "A"] (the circle and diameter) during the Third (Race) and of [see image "B"] during the Fourth.*
>
>This needs explanation. The *diameter*, when found isolated in a circle, stands for female nature, for the first *ideal* World, *self-generated and self-impregnated* by the universally diffused Spirit of Life — referring thus to the primitive Root-Race

also. It becomes **androgynous** as the Races and all on Earth develop into their physical forms, and the symbol is transformed into a circle with a diameter from which runs a vertical line: expressive of male and female, not separated as yet — the first and earliest Egyptian *Tau* [see image "C"]; after which it becomes [see image "D"] or male-female separated [Blavatsky's footnote, "Therefore, putting aside its religio-metaphysical aspect, the Cross of the Christians is symbolically far more *phallic* than the pagan Svastica."] (See first pp. of Book I) and fallen into generation.

Venus (the planet) is symbolised by the sign of a globe over the cross, which shows it as presiding over the natural generation of man. The Egyptians symbolised *Ank*, "life," by the ansated cross, or [see image "E"], which is only another form of Venus (Isis) [see image "F"], and meant, esoterically, that mankind and all animal life bad stepped out of the divine spiritual circle and fallen into physical male and female generation. This sign, from the end of the Third Race, has the same phallic significance as the "*tree of life*" in Eden *Anouki*, a form of Isis, is the goddess of life; and *Ank* was taken by the Hebrews from the Egyptians and introduced by Moses, one learned in the Wisdom of the priests of Egypt, with many other mystical words.

The word *Ank* in Hebrew, with the personal suffix, means "my life," my being, which "is the personal pronoun Anochi," from the name of the Egyptian goddess *Anouki*. [Blavatsky's footnote, "The ansated Cross is the astronomical planetary sign of Venus, 'signifying the existence of *parturient energy* in the sexual sense, and this was one of the attributes of Isis, the *Mother*, of Eve, *Hauvah*, or Mother-Earth, and was so recognised among all the ancient peoples in one or another mode of expression.' (From a modern Kabalistic MS.)"]…

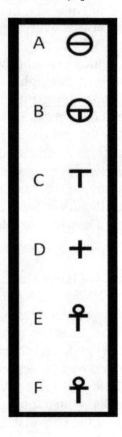

These are the Spirit and Nature, which two form our illusory universe. The two inseparables remain in the *Universe of Ideas* so long as it lasts, and then merge back into Parabrahm, the One ever changeless. "The Spirit, whose essence is eternal, one and self-existent," emanates a pure ethereal LIGHT — a dual light not perceptible to the elementary senses — in the Puranas, in the Bible, in the Sepher Jezirah, the Greek and Latin hymns, in the Book of Hermes, in the Chaldean Book of Numbers, in the esotericism of Lao-tse, everywhere.

In the Kabala, which explains the secret meaning of Genesis, this light is the DUAL-MAN, or the **Androgyne** (rather the sexless) angels, whose generic name is ADAM KADMON. It is they who complete man, whose ethereal form is emanated by other divine, but far lower beings, who solidify the body with clay, or the "dust of the ground" — an allegory indeed, but as scientific as any Darwinian evolution and more *true…*

In one of the most ancient Catechisms of Southern India, Madras Presidency, the **hermaphrodite** goddess Adanari (see also "*Indian Pantheon*") has the ansated cross, the Svastica, the "male and female sign," right in the central part, to denote the pre-sexual state of the Third Race. Vishnu, who is now represented with a lotus growing out of his navel — or the Universe of Brahma evolving out of the central point *Nara* — is shown in one of the oldest carvings as double-sexed (Vishnu and Lakshmi) standing on a lotus-leaf floating on the water; which water rises in a semicircle and pours through the Svastica, "the source of generation" or of the descent of man.

Blavatsky further noted the following regarding symbolism in, Vol. 1, Stanza V:
> The Seven was a Sacred Number with every nation; but none applied it to more physiologically materialistic uses than the Hebrews. With these it was pre-eminently the generative number and 9 the male causative one, forming as shown by the Kabalists the or otz — "the Tree of the Garden of Eden,"[1] the "double **hermaphrodite** rod" of the fourth race. Whereas with the Hindus and Aryans generally, the significance was manifold, and related almost entirely to purely metaphysical and astronomical truths. Their Rishis and gods, their Demons and Heroes, have historical and ethical meanings, and the Aryans never made their religion rest solely on physiological symbols, as the old Hebrews have done. This is found in the exoteric Hindu Scriptures.

Blavatsky's footnote [1]:
> This was the symbol of the "Holy of Holies," the 3 and the 4 of sexual separation. Nearly every one of the 22 Hebrew letters are merely phallic symbols. Of the two letters — as shown above — one, the *ayin*, is a *negative* female letter, symbolically an eye; the other a male letter, *tza*, a *fish*-hook or a dart.

Elsewhere in that section, she has this footnote:
> The sentence in the Sepher Jezirah and elsewhere: "Achath-Ruach-Elohim-Chiim" denotes the Elohim as **androgynous** at best, the feminine element almost predominating, as it would read: "ONE is She the Spirit of the Elohim of Life." As said above, Echath (or Achath) is feminine, and Echod (or Achod) masculine, both meaning ONE.

In, Vol. 1, "IX The Moon, Deus Lunus, Phoebe," Blavatsky wrote:
> This idea of connecting the circle and its diameter line, that is, number ten, with the signification of the reproductive organs…It is *the picture of a double-womb*…This "double womb" also shows the duality of the idea carried from the highest, spiritual, down to the lowest or terrestrial plane; and by the Jews limited to the latter. With them, therefore the number 7 has acquired the most prominent place in their exoteric religion, a cult of external forms and empty rituals; as their Sabbath, for instance, the seventh day sacred to their deity, the moon, symbolical of the generative Jehovah.

While with other nations the number seven was typical of theogonic evolution, of cycles, cosmic planes, and the Seven Forces and Occult Powers in Kosmos, as a boundless whole, whose first upper triangle was unreachable to the finite intellect of man — while other nations, therefore, busied themselves, in their forcible limitation of Kosmos in Space and Time, only with its septenary manifested plane, the Jews centred this member solely in the moon, and based all their sacred calculations thereupon.

Hence we find the thoughtful author of the MSS. just quoted [an "unpublished MSS. on the Art Speech"], remarking, in reference to the metrology of the Jews that: "If 20,612 be multiplied by 4/3 *the product will afford a base for the ascertainment of the mean revolution of the moon*, and if this product be again multiplied by 4/3, this continued product will afford a base for finding the exact period of the mean solar year…this form…becoming, for the finding of astronomical periods of time, of very great service" [the previous two ellipses in original].

This double number (male and female) is symbolized also in some well-known idols: e.g., "Ardanari-Iswara, the Isis of the Hindus, Eridanus, or Ardan, or the Hebrew Jordan, *or source of descent*. She is standing on a lotus-leaf flowing on the water. But the signification is, that it is **androgyne** or **hermaphrodite**, that is *phallus* and *yoni* combined, the number 10, the Hebrew letter *Jod*, the *containment of Jehovah*. She, or rather she-he, gives the minutes of the same circle of 360 degrees"…

In religious rites the moon served a dual purpose. Personified as a female goddess for exoteric purposes, or as a male god in allegory and symbol, in occult philosophy our satellite was regarded as a sexless Potency to be well studied, because it was to be dreaded. With the initiated Aryans, Khaldii, Greeks and Romans, Soma, Sin, Artemis *Soteira* (the **hermaphrodite** Apollo, whose attribute is the lyre, and the bearded Diana of the bow and arrow), *Deus Lunus*, and especially Osiris-lunus and Thot-lunus, [Blavatsky's footnote, "Thot-Lunus is 'Budha-Soma' of India, or 'Mercury and the Moon.'"] were the occult potencies of the moon.

But whether male or female, whether Thot or Minerva, Soma or Astoreth, the Moon is the Occult mystery of mysteries, and more a symbol of evil than of good. Her seven phases (original, esoteric division) are divided into three astronomical phenomena and four purely psychic phases. That the moon was not always reverenced is shown in the Mysteries, in which the death of the moon-god (the three phases of gradual waning and final disappearance) was allegorized by the moon standing for the *genius of evil* that triumphs for the time over the light and life-giving god (the sun), and all the skill and learning of the ancient Hierophants in Magic was required to turn this triumph into a defeat.

It was the most ancient worship of all, that of the *third* Race of our Round, the **Hermaphrodites**, to whom the *male*-moon became sacred, when after the "Fall" so-called, the sexes had become separated. "Deus Lunus" then became an **androgyne**, male and female in turn; to serve finally, for *purposes of sorcery*, as a dual power, to the *Fourth* Root-race, the Atlanteans. With the *Fifth* (our own) the lunar-solar worship divided the nations into two distinct, antagonistic camps.

It led to events described aeons later in the Mahabharatan War, which to the Europeans is the *fabulous*, to the Hindus and Occultists the historical, strife between the *Suryavansas* and the *Indovansas*.
Originating in the dual aspect of the moon, the worship of the female and the male principles respectively, it ended in distinct solar and lunar cults. Among the Semitic races, the sun was for a very long time *feminine* and the moon masculine — the latter notion being adopted by them from the Atlantean traditions. The moon was called "the Lord of the sun," *Bel-Skemesh*, before the Shemesh worship.

Blavatsky's footnote:

During that period which is absent from the Mosaic books — from the exile of Eden to the allegorical Flood — the Jews worshipped with the rest of the Semites *Dayanisi* "the Ruler of Men," the "Judge," or the SUN. Though the Jewish canon and Christianism have made the sun become the "Lord God" and Jehovah in the Bible, yet the latter is full of indiscreet traces of the **androgyne** Deity, which was Jehovah the *sun*, and Astoreth the moon in its female aspect, and quite free from the present metaphorical element given to it.

God is a "consuming fire," appears *in*, and is encompassed *by* fire. It was not only in vision that Ezekiel (viii., 16) saw the Jews "worshipping the sun." The *Baal* of the Israelites (the Shemesh of the Moabites and the Moloch of the Ammonites) was the identical "Sun-Jehovah," and he is till now "the King of the Host of Heaven," the Sun, as much as Astoreth was the "Queen of Heaven" — or the moon. The "Sun of Righteousness" has become a *metaphorical* expression *only now*.

This section also includes the following statement:
> The ancients taught the, so to speak, *auto-*generation of the Gods: the one divine essence, *unmanifested*, perpetually begetting a second-self, *manifested*, which second-self, **androgynous** in its nature, *gives birth in an immaculate way* to everything macro- and micro-cosmical in this universe. This

was shown in the Circle and the Diameter, or the Sacred 10, a few pages back.

Root Races

Blavatsky wrote the following regarding her concept of the *root races* in her book *The Secret Doctrine*, Vol. 2, Stanza IV, "Creation of the First Races":

> Mankinds different from the present are mentioned in all the ancient Cosmogonies. Plato speaks, in the *Phaedrus*, of a *winged race of men*. Aristophanes (*in Plato's Banquet*), speaks of a race **androgynous** and with round bodies. In *Pymander*, all the animal kingdom even is double-sexed. Thus in § 18, it is said: "The circuit having been accomplished, *the knot was loosened*....and all the animals, which were equally **androgynous**, were *untied* (separated) *together with man*....." for...."the causes had to produce effects on earth."
>
> Again, in the ancient Quiche Manuscript, the *Popol Vuh* — published by the late Abbe Brasseur de Bourbourg — the first men are described as a race "whose sight was unlimited, and who knew all things at once": thus showing the *divine knowledge of Gods*, not mortals. The Secret Doctrine, correcting the unavoidable exaggerations of popular fancy, gives the facts as they are recorded in the Archaic symbols [ellipses in original]…

In Vol. 2, "Millions of Years Hence," Blavatsky further notes:

> What is known of other continents, besides our own, and what does history know or accept of the early races? Everything outside the repulsive speculations of materialistic science is daubed with the contemptuous term "Superstition." The wise men of to-day will believe nothing. Plato's "winged" and **hermaphrodite** races, and his golden age, under the reign of Saturn and the gods, are quietly brought back by Haeckel to their *new* place in nature: our divine races are shown to be the descendants of Catarrhine apes, and our ancestor, a piece of sea slime.

Now back to Vol. 2, Stanza IV wherein she references "recent perplexity of the Assyriologists, who express their wonder through the late George Smith" and notes:

> "My first idea of this part" (of the rebellion), he says, "was that the wars with the powers of Evil *preceded the Creation*; I now think it followed the account of the fall" (*Chaldean Account of Genesis*, p. 92). In this work Mr. George Smith gives an engraving, from an early Babylonian cylinder, of the Sacred Tree, the Serpent, man and woman. The tree has seven branches: *three* on the man's side, *four* on that of the female.
>
> These branches are typical of the seven Root-Races, in the *third* of which, at its very close, occurred the separation of the sexes and the so-called FALL into generation. The three earliest Races were sexless, then **hermaphrodite**; the other four, male and female, as distinct from each other.

In the subsection "The Divine Hermaphrodite" Blavatsky delves into her very own home spun anthropology:
> An impenetrable veil of secrecy was thrown over the occult and religious mysteries taught, after the submersion of the last remnant of the Atlantean race, some 12,000 years ago, lest they should be shared by the unworthy, and so desecrated. Of these sciences several have now become exoteric — such as Astronomy, for instance, in its purely mathematical and physical aspect. Hence their dogmas and tenets, being all symbolised and left to the sole guardianship of parable and allegory, have been forgotten, and their meaning has become perverted. Nevertheless, one finds the **hermaphrodite** in the scriptures and traditions of almost every nation; and why such unanimous agreement if the statement is only a fiction?
>
> It is this secrecy which led the Fifth Race to the establishment, or rather the re-establishment of the religious mysteries, in which ancient truths might be taught to the coming generations under the veil of allegory and symbolism. Behold the imperishable witness to the evolution of the human races from the divine, and especially from the **androgynous** Race — the Egyptian Sphinx, that riddle of the Ages!
>
> Divine wisdom incarnating on earth, and forced to taste of the bitter fruit of personal experience of pain and suffering, generated under the shade of the tree of the knowledge of Good and Evil — a secret first known

only to the Elohim, the SELF-INITIATED, *"higher gods"* — on earth only.

Blavatsky's footnote reads "See *'Book of Enoch'*" about which, actually, you can see my book *On the Book(s) of Enoch*.

Blavatsky noted the following in her book *Isis Unveiled* (1877 AD), part I, Science, chap. V:

> But there are myths which speak for themselves. In this class we may include the double-sexed first creators, of every cosmogony. The Greek Zeus-Zen (aether), and Chthonia (the chaotic earth) and Metis (the water), his wives; Osiris and Isis-Latona—the former god representing also ether—the first emanation of the Supreme Deity, Amun, the primeval source of light; the goddess earth and water again; Mithras, [Blavatsky's footnote, "Mithras was regarded among the Persians as the *Theos ek petros*—godof the rock"] the rock-born god, the symbol of the male mundane-fire, or the personified primordial light, and Mithra, the fire-goddess, at once his mother and his wife; the pure element of fire (the active, or male principle) regarded as light and heat, in conjunction with earth and water, or matter (female or passive elements of cosmical generation).
>
> Mithras is the son of Bordj, the Persian mundane mountain [Blavatsky's footnote, "Bordj is called a fire-mountain—a volcano; therefore it contains fire, rock, earth, and water—the male and active, and the female

or passive elements. The myth is suggestive"] from which he flashes out as a radiant ray of light. Brahma, the fire-god, and his prolific consort; and the Hindu *Unghi,* the refulgent deity, from whose body issue a thousand streams of glory and *seven* tongues of flame, and in whose honor the Sagniku Brahmans preserve to this day a *perpetual* fire; Siva, personated by the mundane mountain of the Hindus—the *Meru* (Himalaya). This terrific fire-god, who is said in the legend to have descended from heaven, like the Jewish Jehovah, *in a pillar of fire,* and a dozen of other archaic, double-sexed deities, all loudly proclaim their hidden meaning.

And what can these dual myths mean but the physico-chemical principle of primordial creation? The first revelation of the Supreme Cause in its triple manifestation of spirit, force, and matter; the divine *correlation,* at its startingpoint of evolution, allegorized as the marriage of *fire* and water, products of electrifying spirit, union of the male active principle with the female passive element, which become the parents of their tellurian child, cosmic matter, the *prima materia,* whose spirit is ether, the ASTRAL LIGHT!

In part II, Religion, chap. VI, Blavatsky wrote:
Whenever the Eternal awakes from its slumber and desires to manifest itself, it divides itself into male and female. It then becomes in every system THE **DOUBLE-**

SEXED DEITY, The universal Father and Mother…
IN CHALDEA. The trinity—Anu, Bel, Hoa (or Sin, Samas, Bin), blend into ONE who is Anu (**double-sexed**) through the Virgin Mylitta…

Though he is termed the "Primitive Man," Ennoia, who is like the Egyptian Pimander, the "Power of the Thought Divine," the first intelligible manifestation of the Divine Spirit in material form, he is…neither the male nor female principle, blended into the idea of a **double-sexed** Deity in ancient conceptions, could be comprehended by an ordinary human intellect, the theology of every people had to create for its religion a Logos, or manifested word, in some shape or other…

As the revealed one, he is **Androgyne**, Christos, and Sophia (Divine Wisdom), who descend into the man Jesus. Both Father and Son are shown by Irenaeus to have loved the beauty (*formam*) of the primitive woman, [Blavatsky's footnote, "See 'Irenaeus,' book i., chap. 31-33"] who is Bythos—Depth—as well as Sophia, and as having produced conjointly Ophis and Sophia (**double-sexed** unity again), male and female wisdom, one being considered as the unrevealed Holy Spirit, or elder Sophia—the *Pneuma*—the intellectual "Mother of all things"; the other the revealed one, or *Ophis*, typifying divine wisdom fallen into matter, or God-man—

Jesus, whom the Gnostic Ophites represented by the serpent (Ophis).

In chap. IX, Blavatsky writes:
"Ever ONE, although having *three* forms of double nature (**androgynous**)—he rises! and the priests offer to *God*, in the act of sacrifice, their prayers which reach the heavens, borne aloft by Agni"…

And now, Abel having disappeared out of that line of descent, he is replaced by Seth, who was clearly an afterthought suggested by the necessity of not having the human race descend entirely from a murderer. This dilemma being apparently first noticed when the Kenite table had been completed, Adam is made (after all the generations had appeared) to beget this son, Seth.

It is a suggestive fact that, whereas the **double-sexed** Adam of chapter v. is made in the likeness of the Elohim (see *Genesis* chapter i. 27 and v. 1 of the same), Seth (v. 3) is begotten in Adam's "own likeness," thus signifying that there were men of different races. Also, it is most noticeable that neither the age nor a single other particular respecting the patriarchs in the Kenite table is given, whereas the reverse is the case with those in the Sethite line.

In chap. XII, she wrote:
Esoteric philosophers held that everything in nature is but a materialization of spirit. The Eternal First Cause is latent spirit, they said,

and matter from the beginning. "In the beginning was the word...and the word was God" [ellipses in original]. While conceding the idea of such a God to be an unthinkable abstraction to human reason, they claimed that the unerring human instinct grasped it as a reminiscence of something concrete to it though intangible to our physical senses.

With the first idea, which emanated from the **double-sexed** and hitherto-inactive Deity, the first motion was communicated to the whole universe, and the electric thrill was instantaneously felt throughout the boundless space. Spirit begat force, and force matter; and thus the latent deity manifested itself as a creative energy.

"Jesus clad in woman's clothes"

Blavatsky wrote the following in her book *The Secret Doctrine*, Vol. 1, Stanza III:

> Kwan-Shai-Yin is identical with, and an equivalent of the Sanskrit *Avalokiteshwara*, and as such he is an **androgynous** deity, like the Tetragrammaton and all the Logoi[1] of antiquity. It is only by some sects in China that he is anthropomorphized and represented with female attributes,[2] when, under his female aspect, he becomes Kwan-Yin, the goddess of mercy, called the "Divine Voice."[3] The latter is the patron deity of Thibet and of the island of Puto in China, where both deities have a number of monasteries.[4] (See Part II. Kwan-Shai-Yin and Kwan-yin.)

Blavatsky's footnotes:
[1]
>Hence all the higher gods of antiquity are all "Sons of the Mother" before they become those of the "Father." The Logoi, like Jupiter or Zeus, Son of Kronos-Saturn, "Infinite Time" (or Kala), in their origin were represented as **male-female**. Zeus is said to be the "beautiful Virgin," and Venus is made bearded. Apollo is originally **bisexual**, so is Brahma-Vach in Manu and the Puranas. Osiris is interchangeable with Isis, and Horus is of **both sexes**.
>
>Finally St. John's vision in Revelation, that of the Logos, who is now connected with Jesus — is **hermaphrodite**, for he is described as having female breasts [a citation from Blavatsky would have been useful at this unfounded assertion]. So is the Tetragrammaton = Jehovah. But there are two Avalokiteshwaras in Esotericism; the first and the second *Logos*.

[2]

>No religious symbol can escape profanation and even derision in our days of politics and Science. In Southern India the writer has seen a converted native making pujah with offerings before a statue of **Jesus clad in woman's clothes** and with a ring in his nose.
>
>When asking the meaning of the masquerade we were answered that it was Jesu-Maria

> **blended in one**, and that it was done by the permission of the Padri, as the zealous convert had no money to purchase two statues or "idols" as they, very properly, were called by a witness — another but a non-converted Hindu.
> Blasphemous this will appear to a dogmatic Christian, but the Theosophist and the Occultist must award the palm of logic to the converted Hindu. The esoteric Christos in the *gnosis* is, of course, sexless, but in exoteric *theology* he is **male and female**.

[3]
> The Gnostic Sophia, "Wisdom" who is "the Mother" of the Ogdoad (Aditi, in a certain sense, with her eight sons), is the Holy Ghost and the Creator of all, as in the ancient systems. The "father" is a far later invention. The earliest manifested Logos was female everywhere — the mother of the seven planetary powers.

[4]
> See "Chinese Buddhism," by the Rev. J. C. Edkins, who always gives correct facts, although his conclusions are very frequently erroneous.

An additional statement from this section of *The Secret Doctrine* is:
> In the Egyptian as in the Indian theogony there was a *concealed* deity, the ONE, and the creative, **androgynous** god. Thus *Shoo* is the god of creation and Osiris is, in his original primary form, the "god whose name

is unknown." (See Mariette's Abydos II., p. 63, and Vol. III., pp. 413, 414, No. 1122.)

Darwinian Evolution

Seeking as she did to elucidate *The Secret Doctrine*, Blavatsky pieced information together from any and every source she could and concocted a particular, and peculiar, anthropology and theology. Following are some of her statements regarding an issue I have been focusing on to some extent which is uncovering the occult roots of the postgender movement; a movement to which the transgender movement is merely an open door.

Blavatsky appeals to the worldview philosophy of Darwinian evolution (as opposed to the science of biology) toward the ends of arguing that humanity was originally androgynous or hermaphroditic in p. 109, section "The Tabula Smaragdina - Stanza V - The Evolution Of The Second Race":

> Primeval human **hermaphrodites** are a fact in Nature well known to the ancients, and form one of Darwin's greatest perplexities. Yet there is certainly no impossibility, but, on the contrary, a great probability that **hermaphroditism** existed in the evolution of the early races; while on the grounds of analogy, and on that of the existence of one universal law in physical evolution, acting indifferently in the construction of plant, animal, and man, it must be so.
>
> The mistaken theories of mono-genesis, and the descent of man from the mammals instead of the reverse, are fatal to the completeness of evolution as taught in

modern schools on Darwinian lines, and they will have to be abandoned in view of the insuperable difficulties which they encounter. Occult tradition — if the terms Science and Knowledge are denied in this particular to antiquity — can alone reconcile the inconsistencies and fill the gap. "If thou wilt know the invisible, open thine eye wide on the visible," says a Talmudic axiom.

In the *"Descent of Man"* [Second Edition, p. 161] occurs the following passage; which shows how near Darwin came to the acceptance of this ancient teaching.

> "It has been known that in the vertebrate kingdom one sex bears rudiments of various accessory parts appertaining to the reproductive system, which properly belong to the opposite sex....Some remote progenitor of the whole vertebrate kingdom appears to have been **hermaphrodite or androgynous** [Blavatsky's footnote, "And why not all the progenitive first Races, human as well as animal; and why one 'remote progenitor'?"]...[these last two ellipses in original]
>
> But here we encounter a *singular difficulty. In the mammalian class the males possess rudiments of a uterus with the adjacent passages in the Vesiculae prostaticae; they bear also rudiments of mammae, and some male*

marsupials have traces of a marsupial sac. Other analogous facts could be added. Are we then to suppose that some extremely ancient mammal continued **androgynous** after it had acquired the chief distinctions of its class, and therefore after it had diverged from the lower classes of the vertebrate kingdom?

This seems very improbable, [Blavatsky's footnote, "Obviously so, on the lines of Evolutionism, which traces the mammalia to some amphibian ancestor"] for *we have to look to fishes, the lowest of all the classes, to find any still existent **androgynous** forms.*"

Mr. Darwin is evidently strongly disinclined to adopt the hypothesis which the facts so forcibly suggest, viz., that of a primeval **androgynous** stem from which the mammalia sprang. His explanation runs: — "The fact that various accessory organs proper to each sex, are found in a rudimentary condition in the opposite sex may be explained by such organs having been gradually acquired by the one sex and then transmitted in a more or less imperfect condition to the other."

He instances the case of "spurs, plumes, and brilliant colours, acquired for battle or for ornament by male birds" and only *partially* inherited by their female descendants. In the problem to be dealt with, however, the need of a more satisfactory explanation is evident, the facts being of so much more prominent and important a character than the mere superficial details with which they are compared by Darwin.

Why not candidly admit the argument in favour of the **hermaphroditism** which characterises the old fauna? Occultism proposes a solution which embraces the facts in a most comprehensive and simple manner. These relics of a prior **androgyne** stock must be placed in the same category as the pineal gland, and other organs as mysterious, which afford us silent testimony as to the reality of functions which have long since become atrophied in the course of animal and human progress, but which once played a signal part in the general economy of primeval life...

It is fascinating to read the philosophizing of, both, Darwin and Blavatsky who, at the time they wrote, knew nothing of the information storehouse and replication occurring within the cell, etc.

In fact, she appeals to what has been termed "vestigial organs" which is an evolutionist's manner whereby to say, "What does that organ do? I don't know. Well then, it must be useless and since it is useless, it is evidence that we once used it but no longer do so."

Just as with all supposed vestigial organ proofs of evolution, we know the pineal gland's function now as well as the appendix and many others. See Jerry Bergman and

George Howe's book *Vestigial Organs Are Fully Functional: A History and Evaluation of the Vestigial Organ Origins Concept.*

On p. 180, Stanza VIII, "Evolution of the Animal Mammalians – The First Fall," Blavatsky wrote:
> 31. THE ANIMALS SEPARATED THE FIRST (*into mate and female*) (*b*)....
> [ellipses in original]
> (*a*) Vertebrates, and after that mammalians. Before that the animals were also ethereal proto-organisms, just as man was.
> (*b*) The fact of former **hermaphrodite** mammals and the subsequent separation of sexes is now indisputable, even from the stand-point of Biology. As Prof. Oscar Schmidt, an avowed Darwinist, shows:
>> "Use and disuse combined with selection elucidate (?) *the separation of the sexes*, and the existence, totally incomprehensible, of rudimentary sexual organs. In the Vertebrata especially, *each sex possesses such distinct traces of the reproductive apparatus characteristic of the other*, that even antiquity assumed **hermaphroditism** as a natural primeval form of mankind....[ellipses in original] The tenacity with which the rudiments of sexual organs are inherited is remarkable. In the class of mammals, actual **hermaphroditism** is unheard of, although through the whole period of their development they drag along with them these residues born by *their unknown*

ancestry, no one can say how long ago." [Blavatsky's footnote, "'*Doctrine of Descent and Darwinism*,' pp. 186-7. The 'Unknown Ancestry' referred to are the *primeval* astral prototypes. Cf. § II., p. 260 (*a*)]

A dual being including symbolism such as standing upon the moon.

The Apocryphal Ophiolatreia

Ophiolatreia which has come to be subtitled, "An Account of the Rites and Mysteries Connected With the Origin, Rise, and Development of Serpent Worship in Various Parts of the World" is a literally apocryphal text as the author(s) is unknown, it was published in 1889 AD.

Chap III's contents are listed as including, "Creation and the Phallus—The Lotus—Osiris as the active, dispensing, and originating energy—Hesiod and the generative powers—Growth of Phallic Worship."

It includes the following:
> …the creative power [did] come to be symbolized under the form of the Phallus, in it was recognised the cause of reproduction, or, as it appeared to the primitive man, of creation. So the Egyptians, in their refinement upon this idea, adopted the scarabæus as a symbol of the First Cause, the great **hermaphrodite** Unity, for the reason that they believed that insect to be both male and female, capable of self-inception and singular production, and possessed of the power of vitalizing its own work…

Chap IV states:

> The great **hermaphrodite** first principle in its character of Unity, the Supreme Monad, the highest conception of Divinity was denominated Kneph or Cnuphis among the Egyptians. According to Plutarch this god was without beginning and without end, the One, uncreated and eternal, above all, and comprehending all.
>
> And as Brahm, "the Self-existent Incorruptible" Unity of the Hindus, by direction of His energetic will upon the expanse of chaos, "with a thought" (says Menu) produced a "golden egg blazing like a thousand stars," from which sprung Brahma, the Creator; so according to the mystagogues, Kneph, the Unity of Egypt, was represented as a serpent thrusting from his mouth an egg, from which proceeds the divinity Phtha, the active creative power, equivalent in all his attributes to the Indian Brahma.

Chap V's contents are listed as including, "Rationale of the connection of Solar, Phallic, and Serpent Worship" and states:

> That fire should be taken to be the physical, of what the sun is the celestial emblem, is sufficiently apparent; we can readily understand also how the bull, the goat, or ram, the phallus, and other symbols should have the same import; also how naturally and almost inevitably and universally the sun came to symbolize the active principle, the vivifying power, and how obviously the egg symbolized the passive elements of

nature, but how the serpent came to possess, as a symbol, a like significance with these is not so obvious. That it did so, however, cannot be doubted, and the proofs will appear as we proceed; likewise that it sometimes symbolized the great **hermaphrodite** first principle, the Supreme Unity of the Greeks and Egyptians…

In almost every primitive mythology we find, not only a Great Father and Mother, the representatives of the reciprocal principles, and a Great **Hermaphrodite** Unity from whom the first proceed and in whom they are both combined, but we find also a beneficial character, partaking of a divine and human nature, who is the Great Teacher of Men, who instructs them in religion, civil organization and the arts, and who, after a life of exemplary usefulness, disappears mysteriously, leaving his people impressed with the highest respect for his institutions and the profoundest regard for his memory.

Another dual being including symbolism
such as standing upon the moon.

Matilda Joslyn Gage on Matriarchy, Mound Builders and the Bible

Matilda Joslyn Gage wrote the following in *Woman, Church and State* (1893 AD), chap. I, "The Matriarchate" notes the following within the context of "The ancient Mound Builders of America":

> It is a remarkable fact—its significance not recognized,—that the roughly sketched diameter within the circle, found wherever boys congregate, is an ancient mystic sign[1] signifying the **male and female, or the double-sexed deity**. It is the union of all numbers, the one within the zero mark comprising ten, and as part of the ancient mysteries signifying God, the creative power, and eternal life; it was an emblem of The All…

Jehovah signifies not alone the **masculine and the feminine** principles but also the spirit or vivifying intelligence. It is a compound word indicative of the three divine principles.[2] Holy Ghost, although in Hebrew a noun of either gender, masculine, feminine, neuter, is invariably rendered masculine by Christian translators of the Bible.[3] In the Greek, from whence we obtain the New Testament, spirit is of the feminine gender, although invariably translated masculine.

> The **double-sexed** word, Jehovah, too sacred to be spoken by the Jews, signified the **masculine-feminine** God.[4] The proof of the double meaning of Jehovah, the **masculine and feminine** signification, **Father-Mother**, is undeniable. Lanci, one of the great orientalists, says:
>
> Jehovah should be read from left to right, and pronounced Ho-Hi; that is to say He-She (Hi pronounced He,) Ho in Hebrew being the masculine pronoun and Hi the feminine. Ho-Hi therefore denotes the male and female principles, the *vis genatrix*...[5]
>
> The Hebrew word "El Shaddai," translated, "The Almighty" is still more distinctively feminine than Iah, as it means "The Breasted God," and is made use of in the Old Testament whenever the especially feminine characteristics of God are meant to be indicated.[6]

It is interesting to what conclusions one comes when one's goal is solely to read postgendersism (by any other name) into any and everything.

Gage wrote that "In the Greek" of "the New Testament, spirit is of the feminine gender" and yet, that very texts tells us that "a spirit hath not flesh and bones" (Luke 24:39) and since a spirit, by definition, does not have a body it is not male or female.

It was also stated that "Jehovah should be read from left to right, and pronounced Ho-Hi...He-She...the male and female principles" and yet, she conveniently left out that "Jehovah" is, after all, the *Tetragrammaton*, the four letters, which *Yod Heh Vav Heh* so that Lanci may be one of the great orientalists but can only conclude that Yod Heh Vav Heh is Ho-Hi/He-She by ignoring two of the four letters.

As for *The Breasted God*, it appears to be another case of reading gender when such is not necessarily the case as elucidated by *Blue Letter Bible*:
> Another word much like **Shaddai**, and from which many believe it derived, is *shad* meaning "breast" in Hebrew (some other scholars believe that the name is derived from an Akkadian word *Šadu*, meaning "mountain," suggesting strength and power).

The *Song of Solomon* provides various instances of breasts being likened to something else as is the case with mountain and thus, strength and powder in 4:5 and 7:3, 7-8:
> Thy two **breasts are like** two young roes that are twins, which feed among the lilies…Thy two **breasts are like** two young roes that are twins. This thy stature is like to a palm tree, and **thy breasts to clusters of grapes**. I said, I will go up to the palm tree, I will take hold of the boughs thereof: now also **thy breasts shall be as clusters of the vine**, and the smell of thy nose like apples.

In chap. II, "Celibacy," Gage wrote:
> While the inferior and secondary position of woman early became an integral portion of Christianity, its fullest efforts are seen in Church teachings regarding marriage. Inasmuch as it was a cardinal doctrine that the fall of Adam took place through his

> temptation into marriage by Eve, this
> relation was regarded with holy horror as a
> continuance of the evil which first brought
> sin into the world, depriving man of his
> immortality.

Gage footnotes this statement thusly, "It was a favorite doctrine of the Christian fathers that concupiscence or the sensual passion was the original sin of human nature. Lecky.— *Hist. European Morals*."
A strong qualifying statement is required here as it may be that case that the "Church" (whatever she means by that) at some point viewed women as "inferior" but the Bible affirms that, both, males and females were both created in God's image.

Also, it is somewhat unclear what is meant by Adam's "temptation into marriage by Eve" as they were married, as it were, before the fall into sin. As noted within my book series on *Cain as the Serpent Seed of Satan*, that "concupiscence or the sensual passion was the original sin of human nature" appears to be late dated at best.

Within another footnote Gage claims, "According to Christianity woman is the unclean one, the seducer who brought sin into the world and caused the fall of man. Consequently all apostles and fathers of the church have regarded marriage as an inevitable evil just as prostitution is regarded to-day. August Bebel.—*Woman in the Past, Present and Future*." Again, she quotes an author, in this case a German socialist politician, but not the Bible.

Yes, biblically Eve was beguiled into sinning and Adam followed her lead. However, Gage claims that "According to Christianity woman" actually the one woman Eve, "brought sin into the world and caused the fall of man" however, the Bible actually states, "by one man sin entered into the world, and death by sin; and so death passed upon all men, for that all have sinned" (Romans 5:12) and " by man came death…For as in Adam all die" (1 Corinthians 15:21-22) however, Gage does not complain that *according to Christianity **man** is the unclean one, etc.*

Also, the claim about **all** (mind you) apostles and **all** fathers viewed marriage as such. The fact is that, just as Jesus reiterated it from Genesis:
> And he answered and said unto them, Have ye not read, that he which made them at the beginning made them male and female, and said, For this cause shall a man leave father and mother, and shall cleave to his wife: and they twain shall be one flesh? (Matthew 19:4-5).

Marriage is God ordained and only Paul can be called to question in this regard even though all he states is that he would prefer people to remain unmarried and celibate for the specific purposes of being able to be itinerate preachers. However, if someone cannot handle it, does not have the gift of celibacy, then they should get married (see 1 Corinthians 7, for example).

Gage continues directly from the statement quoted above with:
> The **androgynous** theory of primal man found many supporters, the separation into two beings having been brought about by sensual desire. Jacob Bœhme and earlier mystics of that class recognized the **double sexuality of God** in whose image man was made…

> The more mystical among priests taught that before woman was separated from man, the Elementals were accepted by man as his children and endowed by him with immortality, but at the separation of the **androgynous** body into the two beings Adam and Eve, the woman through accident was also endowed with immortality which theretofore had solely inhered in the masculine portion of the **double-sexed** being.

At the term "the Elementals" Gage's footnote shows that her perspective is derived not from a reading of the Bible but from occultism as she quotes Kabbalists and Theosophists, "Lowest in the scale of being are those invisible creatures called by Kabbalists the 'elementary'…The second class is composed of the invisible antitypes of the men *to be* born."

Gage's footnotes:

[1]
> The phallus and lingum (or lingum and yoni), the point within the circle or diameter within the circle.—*Volney's Ruins*.

[2]
> Observe that I. H. U. is Jod, male, father; "He" is female, Binah, and U is male, Van, Son.—*Sepher Yetzirah*.

[3]
> *The Perfect Way*.—Kingsford.

[4]

> I. A. H. according to the Kabbalists, is I. (Father) and A. H. (Mother); composed of I. the male, and H. the mother. Nork.— *Bibl. Mythol. I*, 164-65 (note to *Sod* 166, 2, 354.)

[5]
> Nork says the "Women clothed with the sign of the Sun and the Moon" is the bi-sexed or male-female deity; hence her name is Iah, composed of the masculine I and the feminine *Ah. Sod.*—Appendix 123.

Well, Nork is biasedly presupposing since the Revelation 12's reference to "Women clothed with the sign of the Sun and the Moon" is not about bi-sexed or male-female but derives its symbolism from Joseph's dream found within Genesis 37.

[6]
> That name of Deity, which occurring in the Old Testament is translated the Almighty, namely El Shaddai, signified the Breasted God, and is used when the mode of the divine nature implied is of a feminine character. Kingsford.— *The Perfect Way*, p. 68.

Versions of highly symbolic illustrations of dual beings.

W. Scott-Elliot's "The Lost Lemuria"

W. Scott-Elliot wrote the following in, *The Lost Lemuria* (1904 AD) section "Processes of Reproduction":
> Sexual or amphigonic propagation (Amphigonia) is the usual method of propagation among all higher animals and plants. It is evident that it has only developed at a very late period of the earth's history, from non-sexual propagation, and apparently in the first instance from the method of propagation by germ-cells…..[ellipses in original] In all the chief forms of non-sexual propagation mentioned above—in fission, in the formation of buds, germ-buds, and germ-cells—the separated cell or group of cells was able by itself to develop into a new individual, but in the case of sexual propagation, the cell must first be fructified by another generative substance.
>
> The fructifying sperm must first mix with the germ-cell (the egg) before the latter can develop into a new individual. These two generative substances, the sperm and the egg, are either produced by one and the same individual **hermaphrodite** (**Hermaphroditismus**) or by two different individuals (sexual-separation).

Like so many others, such as I noted in the chapter on H.P. Blavatsky's subsection on Darwinian evolution, Scott-

Elliot, publishing the above statement in 1904 AD, borrowed from the science (actually, from the worldview philosophy of Darwinian evolution) towards mystical ends. Yet, just as classical Darwinism was replaced with neo-Darwinism and have a plethora of theories jousting for position as the dominant secular worldview philosophy disguised as science; such mystical concepts to have come and gone.

For example, the entire concept of Lemuria, which today is viewed along with Atlantis as an ancient wonder world, was literally invented as a gedankenexperiment as Ernst Haeckel invented it as a mean whereby to explain how lemurs were found in Africa, India, Madagascar and the Malayan Peninsula.

Indeed, it is to Haeckel to whom Scott-Elliot turns quoting his *The History of Creation* (1876 AD, 2nd ed., Vol. I., pp. 193-8):

> The simpler and more ancient form of sexual propagation is through double-sexed individuals. It occurs in the great majority of plants, but only in a minority of animals, for example, in the garden snails, leeches, earthworms, and many other worms. Every single individual among **hermaphrodites** produces within itself materials of both sexes—eggs and sperm.
>
> In most of the higher plants every blossom contains both the male organ (stamens and anther) and the female organ (style and germ). Every garden snail produces in one part of its sexual gland eggs, and in another part sperm. Many **hermaphrodites** can fructify themselves; in others, however,

reciprocal fructification of both **hermaphrodites** is necessary for causing the development of the eggs. This latter case is evidently a transition to sexual separation.

Sexual separation, which characterises the more complicated of the two kinds of sexual reproduction, has evidently been developed from the condition of **hermaphroditism** at a late period of the organic history of the world. It is at present the universal method of propagation of the higher animals......[ellipses in original]

The so-called virginal reproduction (Parthenogenesis) offers an interesting form of transition from sexual reproduction to the non-sexual formation of germ-cells which most resembles it....[ellipses in original]

In this case germ-cells which otherwise appear and are formed exactly like egg-cells, become capable of developing themselves into new individuals without requiring the fructifying seed. The most remarkable and the most instructive of the different parthenogenetic phenomena are furnished by those cases in which the same germ-cells, according as they are fructified or not, produce different kinds of individuals.

Among our common honey bees, a male individual (a drone) arises out of the eggs of the queen, if the egg has not been fructified; a female (a queen, or working bee) if the egg has been fructified. It is evident from this, that in reality there exists no wide chasm between sexual and non-sexual reproduction, but that both modes of reproduction are directly connected.

Dual being before what appears to be a phoenix.

John M. Robertson on Double-Sexed Pagan Deities

John M. Robertson wrote the following in his 1911 AD book, *Pagan Christs* (1911 AD), pp. 296-298:

…the combination of Mithra in a **double personality** with that of a Goddess is made clear, not only by the statement of the Christian controversialist Julius Firmicus, in the fourth century, and later writers, that the Persians make Mithras both **two-sexed and threefold or three-formed**,[1] but by innumerable Mithraic monuments on which appear the symbols of two deities, **male and female**, the sun and the moon, or, it may be, **male and female** principles of the sun or of the earth.

And this epicene or **double-sexed** character is singularly preserved to us in that Mithraic monument of the Græco-Roman period which we possess in our own British Museum, in which the divine slayer of the bull presents a face of perfect and **sexless** beauty, feminine in its delicate loveliness of feature, masculine in its association with the male form.

In such a combination there is reason to see a direct influence of the old Akkado-Babylonian system on the later Mazdean. From the old Akkadians the Semites received the conception of a trinity, the "divine **father and mother** by the side of their son the Sun-God."[2] But their own ruling tendency was to give every God, up to the highest, a "colourless double or wife";[3] and in the final blending of these in a **double-sexed** deity we have the consummation of the idea.

It was not special to Asia; for the Egyptians gave a **double sex** alike to moon, earth, air, fire, and water, making the earth male as rock, female as arable soil; fire masculine as heat, female as light, and so on;[4] and the Greeks and Romans accepted the notion;[5] but it was probably from Chaldæa that it reached the Mithraists. Bel had been represented as both **father and mother** of Enlil, and Belti as both **father and mother** of Ninlil; and there are yet other instances of the Babylonian vogue of the idea of a God **combining the two sexes**. [6]

There is a further presumption that it was either from Babylonia or through Mithraism as modified after the Persian conquest of Babylon that the idea of a **double-sexed** deity reached the Greeks. In the Orphic hymns, which probably represent the theosophy of several centuries before our era, it is predicated of four deities, of whom two, the Moon and Nature (Selenê and Physeos), are normally female, and two (Adonis and Dionysos) normally male.[7] Selenê is further identified with Mên, the Moon-God, who, as being **double-sexed** like Mithra, was finally identified with him in worship and on coins.[8]

As Dionysos and Adonis, originally Vegetation Gods, have at this stage become identified with the Sun, there arises a presumption that a solar cult has been imitated; though at the same time the solar cult may have adopted features from the others. The likelihood is that the notion of a **double-sexed** deity was the outcome on the one hand of the concrete practice of bracketing a male and a female deity together, and on the other hand of speculation on the essence of "divinity." But the concrete process probably came first, and the conjunction of the symbols or heads of a **male and female** deity in one monument or sculpture would give the lead to a mystical theory of a **two-sexed** being.

In "§ 18. Synopsis and Conclusion: Genealogy of Human Sacrifice and Sacrament," Robertson sets out "a tentative genealogical scheme of the history of the sacrificial idea as we have sketched it up to Christianity" which includes:
…there would thus arise the general conception of…C. Human sacrifices, in which the victim (a) represented the God, or (b) had a special efficacy as being a king or a king's son, or (c) a first-born or only son.

In the case of Goddesses, the sacrifice might be a virgin; and this concept would react on the conception of the God in an ascetic movement, making him either **double-sexed** or virtually sexless. For the sacrifice, nevertheless, the victim must latterly be as a rule a criminal. These various victims might or might not be eaten.[2]

Cover of the 1977 edition: note the typical alchemical imagery.

Edward Carpenter "Intermediate Types Among Primitive Folk"

Edward Carpenter's *Intermediate Types Among Primitive Folk* (1914 AD) contains the following elucidation in chap. IV, "Hermaphrodism among Gods and Mortals":

> Jacobus Le Moyne, who travelled as artist with a French Expedition to Florida in 1564, left some very interesting drawings representing the Indians of that region and their customs; and among them one representing the "**Hermaphrodites**"—tall and powerful men, beardless, but with long and abundant hair, and naked except for a loin-cloth, engaged in carrying wounded or dying fellow-Indians on their backs or on litters to a place of safety.
>
> He says of them that in Florida such folk of double nature are frequent, and that being robust and powerful, they are made use of in the place of animals for the carrying of burdens…
>
> Similar stories are told by Charlevoix, de Pauw, and others…It is needless, of course, to say that these were *not* **hermaphrodites** in the strict sense of the term—human beings uniting in one person the functions both of male and female—since such beings do practically not exist.

But it is evident that they *were* intermediate types—in the sense of being men with much of the psychologic character of women, or in some cases women with the mentality of men; and the early travellers, who had less concrete and reliable information on such subjects than we have, and who were already prepossessed by the belief in the prevalence of **hermaphroditism**, leapt easily to the conclusion that these strange beings were indeed of that nature.

De Pauw, indeed, just mentioned, positively refuses to believe in the explanation that they were men dressed as women, and insists that they were **hermaphrodites**!

In 1889, a certain Dr. A. B. Holder, anxious to settle positively the existence or non-existence of **hermaphrodites**, made some investigations among the Crow-Indians of Montana—among whom the Bardaches [which refers to double-spirit, a term that has come to be used by North Americans to denote "gender-variant" people] were called "Boté."

And Dr. Karsch, summarising his report, says 2:—
> "This word, bo-té, means literally 'not man, not woman.' A corresponding Tulalip-word which the Indians of the Washington region make use of is, according to Holder, 'burdash,' which means 'half man, half woman'—and

that without necessarily implying any anomalous structure of the sex-organs…[ellipses in original] The Crow-tribe, in 1889, included five such Boté, and possessed about the same number before…"

The Père Lafitau, whom I have quoted before and who was a keen observer and a broad-minded man, says, in one passage of his *Sauvages Américains*:
"The spectacle of the men disguised as women surprised the Europeans who first landed in America. And, as they did not at all understand the motives of this sort of metamorphosis, they concluded that these were folk in whom the two sexes were conjoined: as a matter of fact our old records always term them **hermaphrodites**"…

…What interests us here is the evidence of the wide-spread belief in **hermaphroditism** current among the early European travellers. That a similar belief has ruled also among most primitive peoples is evident from a consideration of their gods...

The tradition that mankind was anciently **hermaphrodite** is world-old. It is referred to in Plato's *Banquet*, where Aristophanes says:—
"Anciently the nature of mankind was not the same as now, but different. For at first there were three sexes of human beings, not

two only, namely male and female, as at present, but a third besides, common to both the others—of which the name remains, though the sex itself has vanished. For the **androgynous** sex then existed, both male and female; but now it only exists as a name of reproach."

He then describes how all these three sorts of human beings were originally double, and conjoined (as above) back to back; until Jupiter, jealous of his supremacy, divided them vertically "as people cut apples before they preserve them, or as they cut eggs with hairs"—after which, of course, these divided and imperfect folk ran about over the earth, ever seeking their lost halves, to be joined to them again...

I have mentioned the Syrian Baal as being sometimes represented as double-sexed (apparently in combination with Astarte). In the Septuagint (Hos. ii. 8, and Zeph. i. 4) he is called ἡ Baal (feminine) and Arnobius tells us that his worshippers invoked him thus [Thomas Inman, *Ancient Pagan and Modern Christian Symbolism* (1874 AD), p. 119] "Hear us, Baal! whether thou be a god or goddess." Similarly Bel and other Babylonian gods were often represented as **androgyne** [John M. Robertson, *Pagan Christs* (1908 AD), p. 308].

Mithras among the Persians is spoken of by the Christian controversialist Firmicus as two-sexed, and by Herodotus (Bk. i., c. 131) as identified with a goddess, while there are innumerable Mithraic monuments on which appear the symbols of two deities, male and female combined [Ibid., p. 307].

Even Venus or Aphrodite was sometimes worshipped in the double form. "In Cyprus," says Dr. Frazer in his *Adonis*, etc. (p. 432, note), "there was a bearded and masculine image of Venus (probably Astarte) in female attire: according to Philochorus the deity thus represented was the moon, and sacrifices were offered to him or her by men clad as women, and by women clad as men (see Macrobius *Saturn* iii. 7, 2)."

This bearded female deity is sometimes also spoken of as Aphroditus, or as Venus Mylitta. Richard Burton says [*The Thousand Nights and a Night* (1886 AD), vol. x., p. 231]:—

"The Phoenicians spread their **androgynic** worship over Greece. We find the consecrated servants and votaries of Corinthian Aphrodite called Hierodouloi (Strabo, viii. 6), who aided the 10,000 courtesans in gracing the Venus-temple….[ellipses in original]

One of the headquarters of the cult was Cyprus, where, as Servius relates (Ad. Aen. ii. 632), stood the simulacre of a bearded Aphrodite with feminine body and costume, sceptred and mitred like a man. The sexes when worshiping it exchanged habits, and here the virginity was offered in sacrifice."

The worship of this bearded goddess was mainly in Syria and Cyprus. But in Egypt also a representation of a bearded Isis has been found,—with infant Horus in her lap; while again there are a number of representations (from papyri) of the goddess Neith in **androgyne** form, with a male member (erected). And again, curiously enough, the Norse Freya, or Friga, corresponding to Venus, was similarly figured. Dr. von Römer says:—

> "just as the Greeks had their Aphroditos as well as Aphrodite so the Scandinavians had their Friggo as well as their Friga. This divinity, too, was **androgyne**. Friga, to whom the sixth day of the week was dedicated, was sometimes thought of as **hermaphrodite**. She was represented as having the members of both sexes, standing by a column with a sword in her right hand, and in her left a bow."

In the Orphic hymns we have:—
> "Zeus was the first of all, Zeus last, the lord of the lightning;
> Zeus was the head, the middle, from him all things were created;
> Zeus was Man, and again Zeus was the Virgin Eternal."

And in another passage, speaking of Adonis:—

> "Hear me, who pray to thee, hear me
> O many-named and best of deities,
> Thou, with thy gracious hair...both
> maiden and youth, Adonis" [ellipses in original].

Again, with regard to the latter, Ptolemaeus Hephaestius (according to Photius) writes:—

> "They say that the **androgyne** Adonis fulfilled the part of a man for Aphrodite, but for Apollo the part of a wife"...

It is evident that the conception of a double sex, or of a sex combining the characters of male and female, haunted the minds of early peoples.

...there was always a tendency to cultivate and honor **hermaphroditism**, and to ascribe some degree of this quality to heroes and divinities. The other possible reason is that as a matter of fact the great leaders and heroes did often exhibit this blending of masculine and feminine qualities and habits in their actual lives, and that therefore at some later period, when exalted to divinities, this blending of qualities was strongly ascribed to them and was celebrated in the rites and ceremonies of their religion and their temples....

Blavatsky also noted the following in her book *The Secret Doctrine*, Vol. 2, Stanza I, *Beginnings of Sentient Life*, "In the esoteric philosophy it is male and female, or **hermaphrodite**; hence the *bearded* Venus in mythology."

Lastly, Edward Carpenter references an issue that we covered in chapter *Manly P. Hall "man was primarily androgynous"* which you can consult for details:

> And these again are interesting in connection with the account of Elohim in the 1st chapter of Genesis, and the supposition that he was such an **androgynous** deity.
>
> For we find (v. 27) that "Elohim created man in his own image, in the image of Elohim created he him, *male and female* created he them." And many commentators have maintained that this not only meant that the first man was **hermaphrodite**, but that the Creator also was of that nature.
>
> In the Midrasch we find that Rabbi Samuel-bar-Nachman said that "Adam, when God had created him, was a man-woman (**androgyne**);" and the great and learned Maimonides supported this, saying that "Adam and Eve were created together, conjoined by their backs, but God divided this double being, and taking one half (Eve), gave her to the other half (Adam) for a mate."
>
> And the Rabbi Manasseh-ben-Israel, following this up, explained that when "God took one of Adam's ribs to make Eve with," it should rather be rendered "one of his

sides"—that is, that he divided the double
Adam, and one half was Eve…

To reiterate, such fanciful and mystical reinterpretations came about mainly due to Samuel ben/bar Nahman/Nahmani who lived early 3rd c. early 4th c. AD, Maimonides (Rabbi Moshe ben Maimon aka RaMBaM) lived 1135-1204 AD and Rabbi Manasseh-ben-Israel lived 1604-1657 AD.

Azima: Eliphas Levi's simplified
mirror imave of Baphomet.

Donald A. Mackenzie's "Myths of Crete and Pre-Hellenic Europe"

Donald A. Mackenzie noted the following in *Myths of Crete and Pre-Hellenic Europe* (1917 AD), p. 165, chap. VIII, "Pre-Hellenic Earth and Corn Mothers":
> Another mystic conception was that the Great Mother was **bi-sexual**. The Libyan Neith was occasionally depicted as **androgyne**. Isis was the Egyptian "bearded Aphrodite", "the woman who was made a male", as one of the religious chants states, "by her father, Osiris"[James Teackle Dennis, *The Burden of Isis*, p. 49].
>
> The Babylonian Ishtar and the Germanic Freya were likewise **double-sexed**. This idea that deities were abnormal and superhuman applied not only to goddesses…Adonis similarly was "both **maiden and youth**". The Babylonian Nannar (Sin), the moon-god, was **"father" and "mother"** of gods and men.
>
> So was the Syrian Baal. In India Shiva is sometimes depicted with the **right side female and the left male**. The Persian Mithra was a **god and goddess combined**. Herodotus, in fact, appears not to have known that he was other than a female deity. He says the Persians worshipped Urania, "which they borrowed from the Arabians

and Assyrians. Mylitta is the name by which the Assyrians know this goddess, whom the Arabians call Alitta, and the Persians Mithra."

This Michael Maier illustration from the 1617 AD *Atalanta Fugiens Emblem* denotes the *philosopher's stone*. The squared circle is an alchemical symbol which illustrates the interplay of the elements of matter.

Magus Incognito's "The Secret Doctrine of the Rosicrucians"

Magus Incognito (why do I get a distinct feeling that such is a pseudonym?) wrote *The Secret Doctrine of the Rosicrucians* (1918 AD).

The description of Part IV, *The Universal Androgyne* contains the terms, "The Neuter Becomes Bi-Sexual. The Cosmic Hermaphrodite. The Universal Androgyne. Bi-Sexuality in the Universal Manifestation…Phallicism, the Shadow of the Truth. The Symbol of Universal Bi-Sexuality. The Cross and the Circle. The Phallic Cross. The Swastica."

Incognito notes:
> In the Secret Doctrine of the Rosicrucians, we find the following Third Aphorism:
> The Third Aphorism
> III. The One became Two. The Neuter became Bi-Sexual. Male and Female—the Two in One—evolved from the Neuter. And the work of Generation began.
>
> In this Third Aphorism of Creation the Rosicrucian is directed to apply his attention to the conception of the World Soul—the First Manifestation of the Eternal Parent—as a Bi-sexual Universal Being. This Bi-Sexual. Universal Being, combining within itself the elements and principles of both Masculinity and Femininity, is known in the Rosicrucian Teachings as "The Universal

Hermaphrodite," and "The Universal **Androgyne**."

The term "**Hermaphrodite**" is defined as: "An individual which has the attributes of both Male and Female." The term is derived by joining together the two names, viz., Hermes and Aphrodite. The term came into ancient use through the legend of **Hermaphroditus**, son of Hermes and Aphrodite, who, while bathing, became joined in one body with the nymph Salmacis. The term "**Androgyne**" is defined as: "An individual possessing the attributes of both Male and Female; a **Hermaphrodite**." The term is derived from the combination of two Greek words, viz., "Andros," meaning "a man," and "Gyne," meaning "a woman"…

In order to understand the symbology of the Universal **Androgyne**, it is necessary to first become familiar with the two ancient symbols of Sex. In all the ancient philosophies and religions, we find that the "Cross" (+) is the symbol of the Male; and the "Circle" (O) the symbol of the Female In representing the Bisexual, the **Hermaphrodite**, the **Androgyne**, the two symbols, i.e. the Cross and the Circle are combined in one of several ways.
The original way was that of placing the Cross within the circumference of the Circle; but later usage preferred the various forms of the so-called "Phallic Cross," which consists of the Circle, or Oval,

sustaining the Cross which depends downward from it. (See illustrations.) Sometimes the Cross is represented as the letter "T", and the Circle as the letter "O".

Figure 6. Symbol of the Phallic Cross.

Ernest Holmes' New Thought Religious Science

Ernest Holmes (1887-1960 AD) founder of *New Thought* movement based *Religious Science*.

He wrote the following in his 1926 AD book *The Science of Mind*, chapter "Repression And Sublimation" subsection "The Spirit of Sex" and "Man Reënacts the Divine Nature":

> Life is **Androgynous**, i.e., It contains within Itself both the masculine and the feminine factors.
>
> The male and the female of Creation come from One Principle; all come from the One and all will return to the One; all are now in the One and will forever remain in the One...
>
> Man, as we have discussed, reënacts the Divine Nature and makes use of the same Laws that God uses.
>
> We find in man the same **androgynous** nature that we find in God. This nature we call his objective and subjective faculties.
>
> His objective mentality impregnates his subjective with ideas; and in its turn, the subjective, gathering force and energy, projects these ideas into forms.

In the glossary he notes, "FATHER-MOTHER GOD.—The Masculine and Feminine Principles of Being as included in the **Androgynous** One, or First Cause."

If you are interested in my commentary on *Religious Science* in general, see *Religious Science - Science of Mind - Ernest Holmes*.[3]

Being from an alchemical text, this illustration denotes a chemical process. The text reads to the effect of that *hermaphrodite is like a corpse lying in the dark which needs fire.*

Manly P. Hall "man was primarily androgynous"

> *That man was primarily androgynous is quite universally conceded and it is a reasonable presumption that he will ultimately regain this bisexual state.*

Thus wrote Manly P. Hall in his 1928 AD book, *The Secret Teachings of All Ages* chapter "Qabbalistic Keys to the Creation of Man":

> When the plural and **androgynous** Hebrew word Elohim was translated into the singular and sexless word God, the opening chapters of Genesis were rendered comparatively meaningless. It may have been feared that had the word been correctly translated as "the male and female creative agencies," the Christians would have been justly accused of worshiping a plurality of gods in the face of their repeated claims to monotheism!

Hall is overlooking the fact that the "im" ending in "Elohim" is a masculine plural ending (as opposed to the feminine plural ending "ot"). Hall has his own occult, particularly Freemason, friendly perspective which clearly taints his views.
For example, he states, "The plural form of the pronouns us and our reveals unmistakably, however, the pantheistic nature of Divinity." But what has plurality have to do with pantheism (a theology according to everything is the divinity, a part of the divinity, the divinity is everything, everything is the divinity, etc.).

As to our particular context, Manly P. Hall continues:
> Further, the **androgynous** constitution of the Elohim (God) is disclosed in the next verse, where he (referring to God) is said to have created man in his own image, male and female; or, more properly, as the division of the sexes had not yet taken place, male-female.
>
> This is a deathblow to the time-honored concept that God is a masculine potency as portrayed by Michelangelo on the ceiling of the Sistine Chapel. The Elohim then order these **androgynous** beings to be fruitful. Note that neither the masculine nor the feminine principle as yet existed in a separate state!...

To put it as simply as does the Bible, "So God created man in his own image, in the image of God created he him; male and female created he them" (Genesis 1:27). This gives us the newspaper headline version of that which happens and Genesis 2 gives us the elucidation of that event.

> And Adam gave names to all cattle, and to the fowl of the air, and to every beast of the field; but for Adam there was not found an help meet for him.
>
> And the LORD God caused a deep sleep to fall upon Adam, and he slept: and he took one of his ribs, and closed up the flesh instead thereof; and the rib, which the LORD God had taken from man, made he a woman, and brought her unto the man.
>
> And Adam said, This is now bone of my bones, and flesh of my flesh: she shall be called Woman, because she was taken out of

Man. Therefore shall a man leave his father
and his mother, and shall cleave unto his
wife: and they shall be one flesh (Genesis
2:20-25).

As far as we are concerned, Adam was tasked to name the animals for the specific purpose that he would note that there was nothing like himself. Then, Eve is created so as to be his mate; he being male and she being female.

Hall is reading gender into the text so that if Adam and Eve are **androgynous** male-female then God must be as well. Yet, there is no reason to restrict the text to this one issue. For example, theologians have also applied the concept of "in his own image" to God's communicable attributes (such as having volition, a mind, etc.).

Genesis 1 is simply telling us that God created humans "in his own image" and that the humans were, respectably, male and female.

Thus, "the division of the sexes…in a separate state" took place at the onset in that there was no division from a once **androgynous** being. The Bible tells us that God created, both, males and also females in His image.

Further comments by Hall:
> The word ADM signifies a species or race
> and only for lack of proper understanding
> has Adam been considered as an individual.
> As the Macrocosm, Adam is the gigantic
> **Androgyne**, even the Demiurgus; as the
> Microcosm, he is the chief production of the
> Demiurgus and within the nature of the
> Microcosm the Demiurgus established all

the qualities and powers which He Himself
possessed...

Hall references "ADM" due to the Hebrew letters אָדָם
(Strong's H120) the root for which is the same letters with
a different vowel sound (Strong's H119) meaning red,
reddish or ruddy.

It seems that the general term ADM was employed for
"species or race" (both unbiblical terms) and then also of
"an individual." Thus, the male ADM was also named
ADM. Genesis 2:23 states:

> And Adam said, This is now bone of my
> bones, and flesh of my flesh: **she shall be
> called Woman**, because she was taken out
> of Man.

This is stating that ADM stated that the other being was to
be called *'ishshah* (Strong's H802) as she was taken out of
'iysh (Strong's H376). Here, woman and man are different
than the different category of male *zakar* (Strong's H2145)
and female *něqebah* (Strong's H5347) in the same way that
in English we have just those terms: man, woman, male and
female.

Genesis 3:20 states:

> And Adam **called his wife's name Eve**;
> because she was the mother of all living.

So, the female ADM was a woman and was named Eve -
Chavvah (Strong's H2332).

> This is the book of the generations of Adam.
> In the day that God created man, in the
> likeness of God made he him; Male [zakar]
> and female [něqebah] created he them; and
> blessed them, and called their name Adam,

in the day when they were created (Genesis 5:1-2).

Thus, there was the male, man, ADM "Adam" and the female, woman ADM "Eve."

Also, there seems to be that which someone is "called" *qara'* (Strong's H7121) and their "name" *shem* (Strong's H8034) and there is also the cases in which a person is called by a name.

Referencing Genesis, Jesus stated:
> …Have ye not read, that he which made them at the beginning made them male and female (Matthew 19:4)
>
> But from the beginning of the creation God made them male and female (Mark 10:6)

Manly P. Hall delves into deep esotericism via the Kabbalah (or, with a "Q" as he spells it):
> According to the Isarim, the secret doctrine of Israel taught the existence of four Adams, each dwelling in one of the four Qabbalistic worlds…The second Adam…was **androgynous** …The third Adam—likewise **androgynous**—was clothed in a body of light…The fourth Adam was still considered as a single individual, though division had taken place within his nature and two shells or physical bodies existed, in one of which was incarnated the masculine and in the other the feminine potency…

Clearly, these things are being stated so as to buttress mystical notions and not so as to elucidate Biblical theology. In case it may be of interest, see my books *Cain as Serpent Seed of Satan, vol. I*'s chapter "Adam and Eve as Beings of Light Who Were Not from Earth."

Hall then references George Foote Moore's book Judaism which:
>...describes the proportions of the Adamic man:
>>He was a huge mass that filled the whole world to all the points of the compass. The dust of which his body was formed was gathered from every part of the world, or from the site of the future altar.
>
>>Of greater interest is the notion that man was created **androgynous**, because it is probably a bit of foreign lore adapted to the first pair in Genesis. R. [Rabbi] Samuel bar Nahman (third century), said, when God created Adam, He created him facing both ways (פרעופים ויד;) then He sawed him in two and made two backs, one for each figure...

Moreover, Midrash Rabbah is, as its title implies, a compilation of homiletic commentaries. Bereshith (Genesis) Rabbah was compiled circa the early 5th century AD. It states:
>Rabbi Yeremiah, the son of Elazar, said, "When the Holy One—blessed be He!—created Adam, He created him an androgyne, for it is written (Gen. v. 2), 'Male and female created He them.'"

Of course, this is followed immediately with the likewise incoherent statement:
>Rabbi Sh'muel bar Nachman said, "When the Holy One—blessed be He!—created

Adam, He created him with two faces; then He sawed him asunder, and split him (in two), making one back to the one-half, and another to the other."

Again, this is merely Kabbalistic speculation towards mystical ends.

Illustration of a hermaphrodite.

The Androgynous Zodiac

Isaac Myer wrote the following in *The Qabbalah* (1928 AD):

> When the **androgenic** Scorpio-Virgo was separated and the Balance or Harmony made from Scorpio, and placed between Scorpio, i.e., male, and Virgo, i.e., female, then appeared the 32 constellations or signs, as we now have them. The ark is three stories high (perhaps to symbolize Heaven, Man, Earth).
>
> In the figure of the Man, notice the parting of the hair in the middle of the forehead and the arrangement of the beard, whiskers, moustache and the hair, on the back of the neck and shoulders…
>
> We think that the Zodiacal constellations were first ten and represented an immense **androgenic** man or deity…

Within his 1928 AD book, *The Secret Teachings of All Ages* chapter *The Zodiac and Its Signs*, Manly P. Hall wrote:

> Those who hold the opinion that before its revision by the Greeks the zodiac consisted of only ten signs adduce evidence to show that Libra (the Scales) was inserted into the zodiac by dividing the constellation of Virgo Scorpio (at that time one sign) into two parts, thus establishing "the balance" at the point of equilibrium between the ascending northern and the descending southern signs.

(See *The Rosicrucians, Their Rites and Mysteries*, by Hargrave Jennings.)

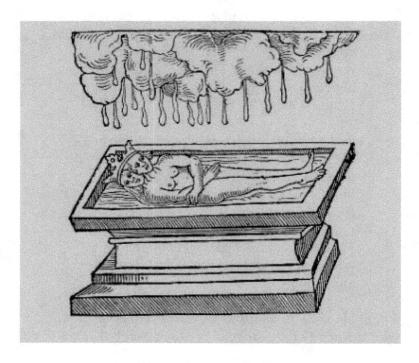

Another illustration denoting alchemical and mystical unions.

The Hawaiian Creation Chant Kumulipo

The Kumulipo - A Hawaiian Creation Chant, as translated and commented upon by Martha Warren Beckwith (pub. 1951 AD), chap. 18, "The Woman Who Sat Sideways" refers to the "second half of the Kumulipo chant" thusly:

…the doubtful opening lines…As written in the text they name Maila, born to La'ila'i when she lived as a woman in the land of Lua; but, if read *O mai la,* where *O* replaces the regular *e* before an imperative, they would summon to a place in the interior of the new home the gods of procreation, the god Kane of the Night-of-multitudes and La'ila'i, the goddess who "sat sideways" to become mother of mankind.

This would be in keeping with Polynesian thought, although we have no confirmation of such an idea in Hawaii. Firth tells us that in Tikopia "structural members of a building" are regarded as "actual embodiments of deity"—hence the fixed positions in the house which were assigned to members of the household.

At the house post sits the male head of the house with his sons and male guests whom he would honor, since the god is considered to be actually present in the stone upon which the post rests, while the women range along the opposite wall.[Firth, *Work of the Gods in Tikopia,* p. 64.]

If this is true for Hawaii, where is the place of *Ki'i ka mahu* in the structural setup? The word *mahú* with the accent on the last syllable is applied to a **hermaphrodite**; it is also given the sense of "quiet." Firth tells us that the Tikopians had gods regarded as **double-sexed**, not in the physical sense but in the sense that, like the Indian god Siva, they were able to show themselves in either a **male or a female body**.

A curious Tahitian chant gives to the god 'Atea such a **shift of sex**, a shift that would, if accepted in Hawaii, explain how Wakea, further on in the Kumulipo chant, lures a water maiden to shore by setting up images (*ki'i*), or why the god Kauakahi, in a folktale from Hilo district on Hawaii, is described as hiding behind an image of a girl until the unsuspecting water nymph of whom he is amorous comes within his grasp. [Firth, *We the Tikopia*, p. 470; Henry, p. 372; Beckwith, Hawaiian Mythology, pp. 540-41]

It is possible that Ki'i, as "image" of the god, has the power of **appearing in either sex**, but I am without evidence that Hawaiians regarded Ki'i as **double-sexed** or whether, if they did so regard him, they would give the name *mahu* to such an attribute. The queen's translation,

> Maila, with Lailai for protection
> And Kane of Kapokinikini was
> support, Kii was helpless,

seems to imply that Ki'i, perhaps representing the danger to a young wife of a misalliance, is one of the evil spirits to be conjured into helplessness. On the other hand, the word *mahu*, unaccented, may apply to a smoldering fire and it would then be possible to think of Ki'i as personifying the fire of sexual passion, with a place in the interior of the house at the oven kept smoldering for quick rekindling, were it not for the fact that Hawaiians built their ovens out of doors and had no need of house fires for heating. The problem hence remains for further investigators, and I take refuge in the more general of the suggested readings.

The Occult Roots of Postgenderism

The Book of Shadows

The so called *Internet Book of Shadows* was compiled from the writings of various authors in 1999 AD. It is a "collection of articles related to Neo-Paganism."

A section titled, "The Manifestation of Kali in Universe as an Astrophysical Anomaly" represents pretty typical Gnostic philosophy/theology and states:

> In the beginning was the KAOS water, the pure creative force of undivided being. [Aleister] Crowley called this "Nuit", which seems to be the combination of the sky goddess "Nut" with the chaos God "Nu", or "Nun".
>
> This was the potential for manifestation before the dream of Siva, before the suffering of Sophia that coalesced into the mist of dark reality.
>
> This primal force exits in a perpetual state of non-being, always edging toward being. A binary movement sets up from this tension of pre-creation, from a state of collapsed oneness, to a state of open potential.
>
> This is the struggle between Siva; the force of perfect order, and Sakti; the force of pure chaos.
> In Siva is the need to collapse to stable systems, the continual drive for one-ness that uni-fests as the point monad of Kether on the Tree of Life.

In Sakti is the need for continual creation,
the pure fertile need to populate Universe
with the divine sparks of manifested
intelligence.
From these two forces arises the numinous
Androgyne.

This force exists at the beginning of physical
creation, from its parthenogenic fullness it
emanates across the Pleroma of the void,
and down the Tree to Malkuth.

This mythos is at the core of the
unconscious and of many creation theories.
From the bliss of **Androgyny** comes the
suffering of Maya, illusion. This is the
illusion of multiverse.

Sophia, the divine mother of the Gnostics,
was conceived of as **Androgynous** but she
broke away from her partner and conceived
the physical universe as a polarized order.
The result was the creation of ignorance, the
demiurge Yahweh.

Postgenderism: Beyond the Gender Binary

Bruce Jenner's sex change operation now known as sex reassignment surgery, the Ethan Hawke movie *Predestination* based on Robert A. Heinlein story ...*All You Zombies*... (1959 AD), Ray Kurzweil virtual reality female alter ego *Ramona*, celebrities popularizing androgynous fashion, new bathroom facilities having to be built or redesigned because some people cannot or do not want to decide whether to enter through the *female* or *male* door, workplace and educational (read, indoctrinational) guidelines being passed regarding *newspeak* manners whereby to refer to non-gender specific personages, etc., etc., etc..

It is of the utmost importance to distinguish between individuals, on the one hand, and movements, on the other. We must be sympathetic to the individual who is genuinely gender confused and is thus, frustrated, confused, bullied and finds it difficult to find their place in the world.

However, within this series is another consideration altogether which is the postgender movement. The movement consists of individuals working through channels of influence within the culture, politics, technology, etc. in order to not only make a place for the aforementioned individual but who seek to radically change the culture for various reasons; a culture made (or rather, remade) in their postgender image. These and many other likewise examples denote a drastic change within the USA's culture and the world's at large.

Under consideration is the paper "Postgenderism: Beyond the Gender Binary" by George Dvorsky and James Hughes, PhD (*Institute for Ethics and Emerging Technologies – IEET Monograph Series*, March 3, 2008 AD). The mere title ought to speak volumes within the context of the facts elucidated above. "Postgenderism: Beyond the Gender Binary" implies, as the paper makes very clear, that the male female *Gender Binary* is something we are going *Beyond* and this is known as *Postgenderism*. As the paper puts it: we are on a "cultural trajectory toward a postgender future."

Genesis 1:27 states, "*So God created man in his own image, in the image of God created he him; male and female created he them.*" With humankind in general as "man" (as in *hu*man) we are told that God created the two genders. Well, everything that Satan does is copying that which God does but turning it inside out, upside down and backward.

As Dvorsky and Hughes note:
> Androgyny was also then adopted by the New Age and transpersonal psychology movements, and melded with the pre-existing cultural and religious ideas about spiritual transcendence of gender (Singer, 1977). The <u>inner spiritual being had both male and female attributes,</u> or was androgynous, and becoming androgynous was <u>spiritually superior</u> to ordinary gendered life.[4]

Beyond naturally occurring eunuchs, androgynous, hermaphrodites and those who chose cross-dressing, the modern, technologically, history of postgendersism is explained as such:

The first male-to-female and female-to-male surgical and hormonal experiments had begun after World War Two, and emerged into the public consciousness when the former US soldier Christine Jorgensen made headline news in the West in 1952 after receiving a sex-change operation and breast implants in Denmark...

It is not surprising that Denmark marks the spot as per, for example, that which I elucidated in the article *Why do*

Atheist countries lead the production of child pornography?[6]

Consider Dvorsky and Hughes's abstract from *Postgenderism: Beyond the Gender Binary* and you will readily discern that there are a lot of things going on behind the socio-political scenes:

> Postgenderism is an extrapolation of ways that technology is eroding the biological, psychological and social role of gender, and an argument for why the erosion of binary gender will be liberatory. Postgenderists argue that gender is an arbitrary and unnecessary limitation on human potential, and foresee the elimination of involuntary biological and psychological gendering in the human species through the application of neurotechnology, biotechnology and reproductive technologies.
>
> Postgenderists contend that dyadic [two individual units, things, or people linked as a pair] gender roles and sexual dimorphisms are generally to the detriment of individuals and society. Assisted reproduction will make it possible for individuals of any sex to reproduce in any combinations they choose, with or without "mothers" and "fathers," and artificial wombs will make biological wombs unnecessary for reproduction.
>
> Greater biological fluidity and psychological androgyny will allow future persons to explore both masculine and feminine aspects of personality. Postgenderists do not call for the end of all gender traits, or universal

androgyny, but rather that those traits become <u>a matter of choice</u>. Bodies and personalities in our postgender future will no longer be <u>constrained</u> and circumscribed by gendered traits, but enriched by their use in the palette of diverse self-expression.

These various concepts will set the stage for this series of articles on postgendersism: technology such as artificial wombs will be employed towards the erosion, elimination of constraint such as to overcome arbitrary limitations from which we must be liberated so as to achieve biological fluidity and psychological androgyny as a matter of choice.

<u>Postgenderism as Transhumanist Technology</u>

We will consider the evolutionary worldview behind the postgender movement which sees our biochemistry, and thus our gender, as being arbitrary. How radical feminism plays into it. That which I will term re-education with regards to gender issues. The ultimate goal(s) of the movement. And transhumanism.

The posthuman movement is active on many fronts, as the paper puts it, "the transcending of gender by <u>social</u> and <u>political means</u> is now being complemented and completed by <u>technological means</u>."

Reference is made to "Homosexuality, Bisexuality, Castration and Cross-dressing – Androgynous," "Hermaphrodites" and "Gender variant people" as constituting "a third sex" and those having "ambiguous genitalia" are viewed as an "intersexuality" an "indeterminate sex" which:

...may now be more prevalent than before due to environmental chemicals that mimic estrogen and interfere with fetal genital development (Dumanoski, Myers, Colborn, 1997).[7]

Other relevant terms of interest are transgender, non-op transsexual, TG butch, femme queen, cross-dresser, third gender, drag king or queen, transboi, omni-gender and pan-gender.

In other words and for example, when a boy's body is literally developing its male characteristic, it is being flooded with pseudo-estrogens and the confused body cannot figure out whether to express female or male characteristics (and genitalia).

Thus, it is noted that "intersex activists," such as the Intersex Society of North America seek:
> ...a postgenderist position, that there is <u>no need to encourage children to ever choose</u> either male or female gender roles. For these intersex radicals, the intersexed are a vanguard of postgenderist rejection of the gender binary.

Moreover, this is no mere accidental byproduct of using plastics, etc. but is being done purposefully via psychopharmacology, neurochemicals, etc.:
> Efforts to treat female depression and male aggression, autism and ADD would give us ways to make the brain more androgynous. Francis Fukuyama lamented these trends, the <u>"masculinizing" of depressive women</u>'s moods by antidepressants, and the <u>"feminizing" of ADD boys</u> with stimulant

> medications, in Our Posthuman Future, asserting that they were the result of pressure to conform to an "androgynous median personality" in American society (Fukuyama, 2002: 52).[8]

Note the reference to "ways to make" as in purposefully setting out to "make the brain more androgynous."

Also:
> Substantial evidence suggests that gender identity, gendered cognition, and sexual preference are shaped prenatally by genes and exposure to testicular and estrogenic hormones (Brizendine, 2007; GIRES, 2008).[9]

And since on a reductionist, naturalist, materialist worldview we are nothing but accidentally conscious combinations of chemicals; what is the difference between one combination or another?

> Technological progress is ameliorating these gender differences...emerging technologies will enable individuals to [chose one or more] gender...genetic and neurological sciences...
>
> Trans- or post-humans would...eventually be able to transcend the biological altogether into cybernetic or virtual form...Greg Egan speculates about such an 'uploaded' society in his novel, Diaspora, where the inhabitants have largely adopted amorphous gender roles, characteristics and the use of gender-neutral pronouns (Egan, 1997)...

But the final liberation from dyadic, gendered, heteronormative relationships will likely come about through use of drugs that suppress pair-bonding impulses. Research with voles has found that genes regulating the neurotransmitter vasopression determine whether male voles will be monogamous or polygamous. Voles with low vasopressin make weak associations between the dopaminergic pleasures of sex and the sight and smell of a particular female, while stronger genes for vasopressin entrains the vole to his female mate.

If similar mechanisms are discovered in the human brain we could eventually have therapies that would allow individuals to turn their pair bonding up or down to a desired level. Some might increase it to block out a wandering eye, while other will turn it down to enable a polyamorous lifestyle…

Many feminists are suspicious of assisted reproduction on the grounds that it is an effort to assert patriarchal technological control over women…

In the 1980s influential socialist-feminist Alison Jaggar" noted that via high tech:
…one woman could inseminate another, so that men and nonparturitive women could lactate and so that fertilized ova could be transplanted into women's or even into men's bodies. (Jaggar, 1983: 132)[10]…

Progress in nuclear transfer from somatic cells into fertilized embryos, and in using somatic cells as <u>faux sperm and eggs</u> to create embryos (Aldhous, 2008) suggest that soon gay and lesbian couples will be able to combine germplasm to <u>make biological children</u>, that individuals will be able to <u>clone themselves</u>, and that <u>three or more parents</u> will be able to contribute germ plasm to <u>create a child</u>.[11]...Once we have perfected tissue cloning and genetic engineering – within the next two decades – we will be able to <u>craft</u> new, fully functional breasts and sexual organs for transsexuals...

...tissue engineering and somatic gene therapies promise much less painful and more complete sex re-assignment (BBC, 2007)...Tissue engineering and nanoneural interfaces suggest that it would be possible to have...some entirely <u>new sexual organ</u>.[12]...

The virtualization of sex, which began with the first cave wall paintings, has been rapid, from widespread access to and use of porn, phone sex, video-interactive sex, sex in virtual worlds, to the eventual perfection of teledildonics, the use of body suits and tactile equipment controlled from afar...One frequent feature of the online world is the crossgender presentation of self, biological men pretending to be women and vice versa (Ludlow, 1996)...In the online world Second Life...participants have a different biological sex than the avatar that they are manipulating.[13]

Moreover:
> When we have our brains laced with nano-neural networks (perhaps in 40 years) we will eventually be able to experience completely virtual body sensation, so we can have sex with partners in virtual reality, or with combinations of virtual reality and material reality (Kurzweil, 2005).[14]
>
> ...researchers in Australia took female mouse embryos with XX chromosomes, and switched on the Sox3 brain gene, resulting in mice with male physiology and behavior (U of Adelaide, 2007).[15]...
>
> Intra-uterine brain gendering, in turn, appears to have some influence on gender identity, gendered behaviors and abilities, and sexual preference...redress the gendering of the brain...
>
> Eventually we will be able to directly stimulate the parts of the brain that desire specific partners or kinds of experiences. We will be able to <u>wire ourselves</u> to only desire sex with the opposite sex, only with our spouse, to only desire specific sex acts, and to desire it according to an agreed upon frequency...
>
> ...a few feminists in the 1970s, such as Shulamith Firestone (1970), had suggested that reproductive technologies could liberate women from biology...[16]

Lastly, as we will consider within the next segment on feminism, reference is made to:

> ...new sub-discipline of "cyborgology" (Gray, 1995) or "cyberfeminism" (Plant, 1998; Sollfrank, 2007) and "technofeminism" (Wajcman, 2004).[17]

The "Feminist Revolution" and Postgenderism

As the title of this article states, we are dealing with the "feminist revolution" as opposed to the "feminist movement," as the paper elucidates as per this quote:

> In her 1970 book The Dialectic of Sex socialist-feminist Shulamith Firestone argued that, just as the material reality of the means of production determined the power differential between the owners and workers, the material reality of women having to bear children determined the gendering of power in society.
>
>> "The heart of women's oppression is her childbearing and child-rearing roles...To assure the elimination of sexual classes requires the revolt of the underclass (women) and seizure of control of reproduction:...so the end goal of the feminist revolution must be unlike that of the first feminist movement, not just the elimination of male privilege but of the sex distinction itself; genital differences between human beings would no longer matter. (Firestone, 1970: 12)"[18]

Thus, the "feminist revolution" views the feminine gender and roles thereof to be oppressive, seek the elimination of sexual classes and, of course, calls for revolt.
These concepts are peppered through "feminist revolution" literature, as the paper elucidates:
> …<u>oppression</u> is her childbearing…<u>burden</u> of childbearing…Women are more <u>impaired</u> in the workforce by <u>pregnancy and childbirth</u>…<u>liberate</u> women from biology…contraception and abortion <u>freed</u> women from being <u>constrained</u> by childbearing…<u>unburdened</u> by the <u>constraints</u> of sex and gender…<u>liberate</u> women from the dictates of reproduction…<u>free</u> them from the necessity of bearing children…<u>freeing</u> them from the neurological gendering of their sexuality.

As per the previous segment on Postgenderism as transhumanist technology, reference is made to:
> …new sub-discipline of "cyborgology" (Gray, 1995) or "cyberfeminism" (Plant, 1998; Sollfrank, 2007) and "technofeminism" (Wajcman, 2004).[19]

Within her 1984 AD essay "A Manifesto for Cyborgs: Science, Technology, and Socialist Feminism in the 1980s," Haraway:
> …argued that it was precisely in the <u>eroding</u> boundary between human beings and machines, in the integration of women and machines into a new <u>liberatory</u> androgynous archetype, that we can find <u>liberation</u> from patriarchy and capitalism. Haraway says "<u>I would rather be a cyborg than a goddess.</u>"

The postgender transhuman "feminist revolution" seeks the "dismantling the heritage of patriarchal power, culture and thought."

Strides in this direction are seen to have been made via "Post-industrial production, contraception and abortion" which "have eliminated most of the rationale for gendered social roles."

> Efforts to ameliorate patriarchy and the disabilities of binary gender through social, educational, political and economic reform can only achieve so much so long as the material basis, biological gendering of the body, brain and reproduction, remains fixed...
>
> During the 1970s the dominant position on nature-nurture among feminists and progressives was "social constructionism" (Delamater, 1998). Patriarchal attitudes and behaviors, gendered differences in abilities and interests, and sexual preferences, were all the result of culturally specific patriarchal and heterosexist socialization. Drawing on Freud, humans were assumed to be naturally "polymorphously perverse," or at least bisexual, until they were conditioned to only respond to heterosexual genital sex.[20]...
>
> Donna Haraway emerged in 1984 as a postgender theorist arguing for technological transgression to liberate both women and men from the gender binary...

...a new "genderqueer" politics emerged which challenged all gender binaries. One critical genderqueer text was the 1990 *Gender Trouble: Feminism and the Subversion of Identity* by Judith Butler. Butler argued that feminists had mistakenly reified the sex/gender binary, while simultaneously insisting that biology was not destiny.

A truly <u>liberatory</u> feminism would seek to <u>deconstruct and free us from the enforced linkages between biological sex, performative gender, and heterosexual desire</u>. She called for intentional subversion of the gender binary – "gender trouble."

Shulamith Firestone articulated in 1971 in favor of artificial wombs as a means to <u>deconstruct the biological basis of patriarchy</u>...

Many feminists are suspicious of assisted reproduction on the grounds that it is an effort to assert <u>patriarchal</u> technological control over women, and of course there is an entirely legitimate critique of maledominated obstetrics behind such a view. However, some feminists have argued that technologies that <u>liberate</u> women from the dictates of reproduction were necessary....

...reproductive technologies give women control over their own biology and potentially <u>free</u> them from the necessity of bearing children.

Pregnancy is the temporary deformation of the body of the individual for the sake of the species. Moreover, childbirth hurts and isn't good for you. At the very least, development of an option should make possible an honest examination of <u>the ancient value of motherhood</u>...

"In the 1980s influential socialist-feminist Alison Jaggar" noted:
> ...the ultimate <u>transformation of human nature</u> at which socialist feminists aim...the capacities for insemination, for lactation and gestation so that, for instance, one woman could inseminate another, so that men and nonparturitive women could lactate and so that fertilized ova could be transplanted into women's or even into men's bodies. (Jaggar, 1983: 132)[21]

The Postgenderism Re-Education of Culture

Many refer to the concept of the slippery slope as being paranoid and yet, the slippery slope is slippery, and is a slope. One example is how words, terminology, language itself is changed so as to fit certain worldviews. Think of the very concept of freedom of speech versus hate speech and you will readily discern this fact.

The paper notes:

Greg Egan speculates about such an "uploaded" society in his novel, Diaspora, where the inhabitants have largely adopted amorphous gender roles, characteristics and the use of gender-neutral pronouns (Egan, 1997).

Keri Hulme proposed a set of gender-neutral pronouns in her book, The Bone People: "ve", "vis" and "ver" (Hulme, 1984).

Today's transgender movement is a roiling, radical critique of the limits of gender roles, with folks living in totally new categories, such as non-op transsexual, TG butch, femme queen, cross-dresser, third gender, drag king or queen and transboi.

These genderqueer activists and theorists advocate postgender attitudes, such as promoting the use of gender-neutral pronouns such as "ze", "per", and "zir," or the terms pansexual or omnisexual instead of the binary "bisexual."

One can discern how far beyond this we have gone as, for example, in 2014 AD Facebook offered users the option of self-identifying as any of 71 genders.

Note the evolutionary premise:
> A mounting body of ethological and sociobiological research suggests that both human males and females, like our primate and mammal cousins, are genetically inclined to have multiple partners. Even those few species that have been thought to

be monogamous and pairbonded for life are now being found to have a high frequency of off-spring not related to the putative father (Barash and Lipton, 2001).

Based on all this evidence Helen Fisher writes in Anatomy of Love that the <u>primordial human "blueprint" is for serial sets of pair bonds lasting about four years</u> — long enough to raise a child to toddlerhood — with clandestine adultery on the side.

The majority of all human societies have been polygamous (Wilson, 1992), and in most monogamous cultures men, at least, have been allowed to pursue extramarital relationships such as concubinage, prostitution, and mistresses.[22]

The paper refers to "<u>social, educational, political and economic reform</u>…by <u>social and political means</u>" so as to get "Beyond Gender Essentialism and Constructionism."
>…as part of a general <u>postgendering of society</u>, the gradual accumulation of neurotechnologies which allow for <u>remediation</u> sexual preference and the gendered brain will <u>complete the postgenderist trajectory</u>.

The paper notes:
>…philosopher Peter Singer, who argued in *A Darwinian Left: Politics, Evolution, and Cooperation* (2001) that there is a biologically rooted tendency towards selfishness and hierarchy in human nature

which has defeated attempts at egalitarian social reform.

If the Left program of social reform is to succeed, Singer argues, we must employ the new genetic and neurological sciences to identify and modify the aspects of human nature that cause conflict and competition.

Note that he seeks to "modify the aspects of human nature that cause conflict and competition" by exercising aspects of human nature that cause conflict and competition by causing conflict and competition in proposing to modify certain aspects of human nature, in part, in opposition to those who do not agree with postgenerism.
Moreover:

> ...psychologists such as Sandra Bem (1974), the developer of the Bem Sex Role Inventory, began to reconceptualize gender traits as a continuum, along which it was healthiest to be in the androgynous range. The androgynous had the highest self-esteem, psychological well-being and emotional intelligence, while those at the psychological extremes of gender were re-cast as constrained and disabled (Guastello and Guastello, 2003).[23]

Here you can see that the deterioration of traditional marriage (by heterosexual divorces, same sex "marriage," etc.) is also being done on purpose:

> The spread of legal gay marriage in Europe, and its slower adoption in the US, has accelerated the recognition of legal marriage as an arbitrary contract, rather than a religious, heterosexual, dyadic institution.

Therefore laws against polygamy and group marriages must eventually fall, since they are clearly based in religious discrimination.

Eventually co-housing and co-parenting "civil union" contracts <u>should</u> replace civil marriage. Those contracts would recognize the bonds between small groups of people who have made commitments of some duration. <u>The erosion of dyadic marriage will, in turn, help to erode the gender binary.</u>

The Postgenderism Worldview and Literature

We have already noted, in passing, that since on a reductionist, naturalist, materialist worldview we are nothing but accidentally conscious combinations of chemicals; what is the difference between one combination or another?

Note the evolutionary premise in, for example, referring, as the paper does, to "<u>Biological</u> gender dimorphism" (existence of two or more different forms within a biological species aka female and male).

There are, of course, also references to "our <u>accidental</u> binary gender assignments (Geary, 2006; Ridley, 2003)."[24]

So our binary gender is the byproduct of accidental biology, as per this particular and peculiar worldview. Here is some more from the paper:
> Today however, our Enlightenment values and emergent human potentials have come into conflict with the <u>rigid gender binary</u>.

Efforts to ameliorate patriarchy and the disabilities of binary gender through social, educational, political and economic reform can only achieve so much so long as the material basis, <u>biological gendering</u> of the body, brain and reproduction, remains fixed.

…the <u>transcending of gender</u> by social and political means is now being complemented and completed by technological means.

Technological progress is ameliorating these gender differences, but only the blurring and erosion of biological sex, of the gendering of the brain, and of <u>binary social roles</u> by emerging technologies will enable individuals to access all human potentials and experiences regardless of their born sex or assumed gender.

Some "Intersexual characters" references within the paper are found within the following texts:

Charlotte Perkins Gilman, *Herland* (1915 AD) according to which, "women reproduce parthenogenetically and only have daughters."

"The idea of female-only reproduction" is also found within Joanna Russ, *The Female Man* (1975 AD) and Suzy McKee Charnas' *Motherlines* (1978 AD) and *The Furies* (1995 AD).

Ursula K. LeGuin, *Left Hand of Darkness* (1969 AD), "depicts a society that has engineered itself to be neuter for most of each month, except for a period of heat in which they become either male or female."

Lois McMaster Bujold, *The Miles Vorkosigan* series "has a hermaphrodite character from a postgender society that has intentionally genetically engineered itself so that all its members are hermaphrodites."

Jeffrey Eugenides, *Middlesex* (2002 AD; this destruction of traditional gender and roles made it into Oprah's Book Club) features, "chromosomally male but appears to have a vagina, and is raised as a girl until becoming male as an adolescent."

Ian McDonald, *River of Gods* (2004 AD):
>...proposes a new sexual identity and subculture, neuters or "nutes," that evolve out of the hijra cult in India, and whose members have their external sex organs surgically redesigned into a smooth androgynous form, whose brains are genetically adjusted to an androgynous condition, and who are given a set of internal controls over their sexual responses which have a broader range than male or female orgasms.

Gender issues considered from a Judeo-Christian perspective are:
Alexander Strauch, *Men and Women, Equal Yet Different: A brief study of the Biblical Passages on Gender* (1999 AD).

John Piper and Wayne Grudem, *Recovering Biblical Manhood and Womanhood: A Response to Evangelical Feminism* (2012 AD).

George W. Knight III, *Role Relationships of Men and Women: New Testament Teaching* (1989 AD)

More alchemical symbolism of combination.

Intro to the Appendices

From the *Postgenderism Worldview and Literature* section, it should be evident that obscure fictional books and obscure journal papers are being appealed to with much more import than any obscure work would otherwise deserve.

This fact appears to be a window into echo chambers within academe's imitation ivory towers. That which occurs beyond the halls of learning is viewed as a vast experiment and that which occurs within becomes a vicious cycle of confirmation bias.

In part, this is due to those within considering themselves to be the erudite class, the technocrats as it were, who are talking natural selection away from blind unguided nature and have appointed themselves as unnatural selectors who will guide humanity into the next phase of human design, not evolution, or rather, redesign: a humanity after our own image.

The Bible states, "a little child will lead them" (Isaiah 11:6) within, that is, the context of the domestication of previously wild, ravenous animals, "The wolf shall dwell with the lamb, and the leopard shall lie down with the young goat, and the calf and the lion and the fattened calf together; and a little child shall lead them."

Culture de jour is telling us that "a little child will lead them" with "little child," statistically speaking, referring to children who are confused, undergoing a phase, have suffered trauma, etc. and "them" being the rest of, over 99%, of society.

We are allowing mere children to decide to get locked into a lifetime of taking hardcore pharmaceuticals and undergoing radical surgery that will literally change them from the inside. This is generally based on what may be a whim de jour or the side effect of trauma through which they would otherwise be helped to work speaks for itself. That we have adults, such as their parents, not only allow it but introduce the concept of such drugs and surgery to them—and then championing their lifestyle choices along with the changing of federal and local laws which comes with, in terms of special protections, etc.

Within these appendices I will evidence the fact that we are told that—let us pause a moment. We often hear that as a society we should have various "conversations" but these never manifest. Rather, we are told, ordered, what will be and anyone who disagrees is besmirched via various terms. Thus, we have had no conversation about the manner whereby society is being radically transformed but we are simply *told* that it will be and how it will be.

That upon which I will focus is that we are *told* that the science behind psychiatry and psychology results in that, for example, homosexuality is no longer a mental disorder as it was thought for many decades.
However, when one reads the history of such shifts in *science* at least one thing is crystal clear.
As per a hard science such as generics (I am referring to the *mathematical* aspect of genetics): male genetics are male genetics and female genetics are female genetics (and I am granting that there are some rare cases of genetic abnormalities).
As per soft science psychiatry and psychology (referring to highly reliant on interpretation and even though neuroscience is being employed into those fields there is still an aspect of neuroscience which interprets lights on a

screen): gender is a social construct based on feelings (which is why one's gender can change from day to day).

Now, what is readily discernable when considering the history of the *scientific revolution* regarding gender as per psychiatry and psychology the hard science has not changed in the least bit. Rather, it is openly admitted that such changes are based on socio-political activism: as the culture goes so does the alleged science—which is *science* only so called.

This way of being led by children is a result of those children, in turn, being influenced by childish adults (and bio-social engineers, remember the reference to "ways *to make* the brain more androgynous"). In a manner of speaking, this is the ultimate result of obvious (and also engineered) *dumbing down*. For example, public schooling tells us *what* to think but does not teach us *how* to think. Now, when people are dumbed down they do not develop cognitive abilities whereby to intellectually handle complex issues employing logic, incorporating data points, discerning logical conclusions, etc.
Rather, dumbed down people are left to deal with and based their views on emotions. Anyone and everyone has emotions but not everything is well developed cognitive abilities.

This is whence comes the issue we currently face which is that *if it feels good, do it* (a mere reworking of Aleister Crowley's *do what thou wilt*) so that if you have an intellectual point to make it cannot compete against an emotion. This is because an emotion is actually felt whilst in comparison intellectual points come across as being abstract.

This is why a child's feeling—fleetingly tentative as they are—are not being allowed to be overcome by facts, logic, science, etc.

As noted in this work's introduction, the free sex sexual revolution opened the door to homosexuality which opened the door to transgenderism which is opening the door to postgendersism and all of it has as its ultimate target the last vestige of societal, and thus personal, stability: the traditional family.

Appendix: Dr. Phil McGraw

This appendix proceeds forth from my book *In Consideration of Rev. Dr. Mel White on Christian Homosexuality*. I am referring to Dr. Phil McGraw as he is a psychologist with decades of experience, enough time to have seen many changes within that field, and because he is immensely influential.

These are some note that I took from watching a *Dr. Phil Show* episode which aired on April 1, 2013 AD.

Sadly, it was not an *April Fool's Day* joke; although it was foolish. The show was titled, "Shocking Mom Revelations":

> Doreen, 26, says she realized she was gay at a young age and that her mother, Diane, doesn't accept her relationship with her girlfriend, Ana.

One of the reasons they emphasized the mom's disapproval is, "Diane says she blames softball for Doreen's 'choice' to be gay." Thus, the question is posed, "Can Dr. Phil help build a bridge of acceptance?" so his point is, solely, to have the mom "accept" homosexuality.

Well, the mom noted that homosexuality is against God's will. Dr. Phil then assured her that he too is a Christian but that now we have decades of research behind us and now we know _____ (fill in the blank with the proclamations de jour of researchers).

Wow, if only God would have known that which Dr. Phil knows.
He assures her that she is "dead wrong" because his field of psychology, which is based on viewing humans are haphazardly evolved bio-organisms, has uncovered that homosexuality is perfectly normal, natural, etc.

The mom affirms that homosexuality is a choice; which it is, of course (one may have a "born this way" impulse—which is original sin—but one chooses to turn impulse into action/activity/lifestyle).

Dr. Phil notes that homosexuality is "natural" for the daughter and attempting to make her change would be like attempting to make a heterosexual become homosexual.

The mom noted that there are ex-homosexuals which there are, of course (Joe Dallas, for example, who has written various books on this issue).
Dr. Phil denied this noting that they must not have really been homosexual—because, apparently, no true homosexual would ever change (*True Scotsman* fallacy anyone?).

Note the tactic which Dr. Phil is employing: by claiming that ex-homosexuals must not have really been homosexual he, by fiat, makes evidence of homosexual becoming ex-homosexuals literally impossible.
Any number of such cases could be provided to Dr. Phil and he could simply wave them off by stating that they must not have really been homosexual. This is, both, unscientific and illogical.

The reason that merely noting that it is against God to be homosexual does not go far enough is that homosexual

activists (and their heterosexual supporters) argue that "natural" is in the eye of the beholder.
Thus, heterosexuality is natural for the heterosexual and homosexuality is natural for the homosexual.

The deeper issue is that God invented sexual relationships, did so within the confines of a one man, one woman marriage and that, He sets the standard for what is "natural." That the "natural man" thinks otherwise is only indicative of the noetic effects of the fall, "But a natural man does not accept the things of the Spirit of God, for they are foolishness to him; and he cannot understand them, because they are spiritually appraised" (1 Corinthians 2:14). Here "natural" is defined by the context, of course.

Dr. Phil's point is that it is wrong to expect homosexuals to restrict, suppress, deny or attempt to change their nature. Yet, there are myriads of personages who most certainly ought, should and must restrict, suppress, deny and attempt to change their nature and we demand that they do so under threat of imprisonment or even capital punishment. When his argument fails when applied to anyone else then you know that it is fallacious.

Dr. Phil notes that as recently as the 1970s AD homosexuality was categorized, by psychologists/psychiatrists, as a mental disorder. Yet, today we know so much more. So, psychologists/psychiatrists told us one thing and now another; apparently, we are supposed to just go along with their preferred theories de jour.

Thus, if you take Dr. Phil's theory/argument in favor of homosexuality's natural normalcy and apply it to various other activities, including other sexual practices, they utterly fail.

This is proof that he is playing a PC, PR game which sets the knowledge of man, psychology/psychiatry, against the knowledge of God.

Subsequently, Dr. Phil has featured a very, very troubled woman who purposefully blinded herself because she self-identified as blind and felt like a blind person in an sighted person's body.
Dr. Phil rightly noted that the therapists to which she spoke about how to go about blinding herself were unethical for advising her. Yet, when it comes to removing or fundamentally changing a sexual organ, he does a 100%, 180° turn and thinks that it is ethical and healthy.

He also featured Rachel Dolezal who is "White" but self-identified as "Black." Dr. Phil pointed out various ways in which she was simply and factually wrong and that she deceived people for claiming that she was "Black" when she is not. However, he does a 100%, 180° turn when a person of one gender claims that they are of another gender.

Appendix: History of Homosexual Socio-Political Psychiatric Activism

Jack Drescher, M.D., who is a psychiatrist and psychoanalyst, compiled some interesting data with regards to, as he states it within his relevant paper's title, "Queer Diagnoses: Parallels and Contrasts in the History of Homosexuality, Gender Variance, and the Diagnostic and Statistical Manual" which was published in the *Archives of Sexual Behavior*, April 2010 AD, Volume 39, Issue 2, pp 427-460. I will add bold and underlining emphasis for emphasis.

Interestingly, he cites John Godfrey Saxe's "The Blindmen and the Elephant" tale which concludes the following about the blind men attempting to identify the elephant and coming to different conclusions, "each was partly in the right / And all were in the wrong." He analogizes this with views of homosexuality as an assertion about how any view of homosexuality is not likely to be holistic but partial.

Activists argued, as in the case of homosexuality in the 1970s, that it is wrong to label expressions of gender variance as symptoms of a mental disorder and that perpetuating DSM-IV-TR's GID diagnoses in the DSM-V would further stigmatize and cause harm to transgender individuals.
FYI: DSM refers to the *Diagnostic and Statistical Manual* and GID to *Gender Identity Disorders*.

Note a recurring theme which is that much of what has occurred within psychiatry (the study and treatment of mental illness, emotional disturbance, and abnormal behavior) and psychology (the scientific study of the human mind and its functions, especially those affecting behavior in a given context) is based on sociopolitical activism and philosophical arguments. In this case, a moral assertion was made that, "it is wrong" because it would "further stigmatize and cause harm." Thus, apparently, psychoanalysis are to base their conclusions nor upon science but upon the most vociferous arguments de jour.

Drescher also relates the view that "As in the case of homosexuality in the 1970s, **it is wrong** for psychiatrists and other mental health professionals to label expressions of gender variance [Drescher's footnote, "Following Meyer-Bahlburg (2009), 'The nomenclature in the area of gender variations continues to be in flux, in regard to both the descriptive terms used by professionals, and, even more so, the identity terms adopted by persons with GIV [Gender-Identity-Variants].' Where possible, this author will use the term 'gender variance' to refer to individuals with gender atypical behavior or self presentations"] as symptoms of a mental disorder."

In fact, he specifically refers to "scientific and clinical etiological theories that **implicitly moralize** about matters of sexuality and gender" with reference to etiology which is the branch of medicine that investigates the causes and origins of disease. Also, Robert Stoller, M.D. is quoted to the effect that, "We are in a new era in which diagnosis has…social and political implications."

Also, Drescher states, "many, if not all, diagnostic categories have a social context." For that matter, he also states:

Some have sought to discredit psychiatric diagnoses, regardless of their clinical utility, because all diagnoses are subjective and argue that psychiatric nosology is at best a "soft science" and, at worst, not a science at all. Yet the criticism of "subjectivity" can apply to even the "hardest" of sciences, as when the International Astronomical Union recently decided, by a membership vote, that Pluto is no longer a planet.

Of course, this is more like an excuse of sorts as psychiatry is mostly worldview based interpretations of observed behaviors, etc. Drescher also refers to "psychiatric theorizing" and to "the field of queer theory."

This is nothing new as, for example, Drescher notes that in 1935 AD Sigmund Freud wrote:

> Homosexuality is assuredly no advantage, but it is **nothing to be ashamed of, no vice, no degradation**; it cannot be classified as an illness; we consider it to be a variation of the sexual function, produced by a certain arrest of sexual development.

Drescher adds, "Yet, by the early 20th century, psychiatrists mostly regarded homosexuality as pathological." For example:

> ...the first edition of the DSM (APA, 1952) explicitly and non-self consciously articulated a role for social values in making a diagnosis of the overarching category of sociopathic personality disturbances which included homosexuality:
>
> > "Individuals to be placed in this category are ill primarily in terms of

> society and conformity with the
> prevailing cultural milieu, and not
> only in terms of personal discomfort
> and relations with other individuals."

Drescher notes that in the 1970s AD, "a common psychiatric belief that saw trans people as severely mentally disturbed." It was in 1973 AD that the "APA's Board of Trustees (BOT) voted to remove homosexuality from the DSM." Also, some pondered, "What role should APA and the DSM play in **changing society's attitudes** toward transgenderism?"

Thus ended the American classification of homosexuality per se as an illness. Within two years, other major mental health professional organizations, including the American Psychological Association, the National Association of Social Workers, and the Association for Advancement of Behavior Therapy, endorsed the APA decision.

It is noted that "Clinical efforts with gender variant children aimed at getting them to reject their felt gender identity and to accept their natal sex were" not only "unscientific" but also "unethical."

> By the late1990s, as trans inclusion became
> a focus of LGBT civil rights organizations...
> Like the gay community that argued to be
> taken out of an earlier diagnostic nosology,
> the trans community has adopted similar
> **normalizing arguments** to make the case
> for removal. These include... **adopting** and
> **insisting upon** the use of **normative**
> **language** to **replace medical terminology**
> ("homosexuals" become gay or defiantly
> queer; "gender dysphoria" becomes gender

dissonance; "gender reassignment surgery" becomes gender confirmation, gender affirmation surgery, genital reassignment surgery, or bottom surgery);
• labeling theories that **contradict affirmative perspectives as unscientific**;
• **ad hominem and ad feminam attacks on professionals** who either believe homosexuality/transgenderism is an illness or use pathologizing language to make sense of homosexuality/transgenderism.

This is of the utmost importance as there is a behind the scenes activist effort to normalize homosexuality in its various forms by a form of re-education based on Orwellian thought policing of newspeak via monitoring and changing terminology: not only taking it upon oneself to be aware of "adopting" normative language but "insisting upon" as in demanding that others do so as well.

We are now in a new McCarthyism era the point of which is not to make attempts, however misguided or manipulated, to root out Communism which caused the deaths of hundreds of millions of people but so as to root out those who consider homosexuality to be abnormal, unethical, wrong, sinful, etc.

This is tantamount to the point made within the subsection above on the *Postgender Re-education of Culture*.

But the deeper point is to note that the normative-newspeak-language which is based on homosexual mores is meant to "replace medical terminology" the result of which is that "theories that contradict affirmative perspectives," that is any scientific theory that contradicts the affirmation of homosexuality as normal, natural, ethical, etc., is to be labeled as "unscientific" not on scientific grounds but solely on the basis that it does not affirm homosexuality to be normal, natural, ethical, etc.

More militant still, calls are made for ad hominem and ad feminam attacks. Now, ad hominem ad feminam means to the man or woman and is a logical fallacy whereby one aims one's attack (counter argument or answer) to the person whilst leaving the original argument or question unscathed. It is a fallacious manner whereby to attempt to divert the debate from the issue at hand to the persons making the arguments or asking the questions.

Now, in this case the militants call for illogical besmirching of "professionals," not on a scientific basis but solely based on whether the professionals "believe homosexuality/transgenderism" to be "an illness" or that they "use pathologizing language"; this is no less than a form of censorship and the politics of personal destruction.

Drescher points out:
> Several years ago, members of the LGBT community protested the content of Northwestern University's J. Michael Bailey's (2003) book, The Man Who Would be Queen. While there were activists who primarily criticized the author's arguments regarding transgenderism, some activists **attacked Bailey's character, reputation, and family members**.

Some homosexuals are now working from within psychiatric organizations:
> …there are **hundreds of openly LGB psychiatrists advocating** for organizational awareness of LGB rights, both within APA

as well as in its allied organization, the Association of Gay and Lesbian Psychiatrists (AGLP). There are very few visible trans psychiatrists within either organization.
The Committee on Gay, Lesbian, and Bisexual Issues often functioned as the default clearinghouse for queries to the APA about trans issues.

Drescher notes the following of homosexuality's "transgender wing" who were "striving for suburban normalcy":

> The change is fueled **mostly** by a **community of parents** who, like many parents of **this generation**, are open to letting even **preschool children define their own needs**. Faced with skeptical neighbors and school officials, parents at the [Trans Health] conference discussed how to use the kind of **quasi-therapeutic language** that, these days, inspires deference: tell the school the child has a "medical condition" or a "hormonal imbalance" that can be treated later, suggested a conference speaker, Kim Pearson; using **terms** like gender-identity disorder or birth defect would be going too far, she advised.
>
> The point was to **take the situation out of the realm of deep pathology or mental illness**, while at the same time separating it from voluntary behavior, and to put it into the **idiom** of garden-variety "challenge."

Yet, beyond merely appealing to personal moral preferences and Orwellian newspeak, Drescher notes that "Like an earlier generation of gay activists who **turned to scientific findings to support their movements normalizing arguments**":

> There have also been studies that have examined a small, sexually dimorphic region of the brain known as the BSTc. Researchers found that the structure of the BSTc region in trans women more closely resembles that of most women, while in trans men it resembles that of most men [Garcia-Falgueras & Swaab, 2008; Kruijver et al., 2000; Zhou, Hofman, Gooren, & Swaab, 1995].
>
> Like all brain research, such studies have certain limitations and caveats, but they do suggest that our brains may be hardwired to expect our bodies to be female or male, independent of our socialization or the appearance of our bodies (Serano, 2007, p. 81).

That "the BSTc region in trans women more closely resembles that of most women, while in trans men it resembles that of most men" implies that homosexuals cannot appeal to it since it is virtually the same in trans personages as well as heterosexuals.

Drescher tries his hand at scientific support:
> We find that the prevalence of SRS is at least on the order of 1:2500, and may be twice that value. We thus find that the intrinsic prevalence of MtF transsexualism

must be on the order of 1:500 and may be
even larger than that.

Note the utter folly of his attempt as the works with a number that is either one ratio or else "twice" as much. Yet, upon such a vague ration the concluded that "thus" the result is either one ratio or another that is "even larger."

The 2012 AD DSM-V:
> ...generated a flurry of concerned and anxious responses in the lesbian, gay, bisexual, and transgender (LGBT) community and blogosphere, mostly focused on the status of the diagnostic categories of Gender Identity Disorder (GID) of Adolescence and Adulthood and GID of Childhood (GIDC).

Drescher was a member of the DSM-V Work Group on Sexual and Gender Identity Disorders.

More comments on socio-political premises follow:
> As in the case of homosexuality, arguments for removal of the "trans diagnoses" include **societal intolerance** of difference, the human cost of diagnostic stigmatization, using the language of psychopathology to describe what some consider to be normal behaviors and feelings and, finally, inappropriately focusing psychiatric attention on individual diversity rather than opposing the social forces that oppress sexual and gender nonconformity.

Moreover:

...**the most significant** catalyst for diagnostic change was **gay activism**. In the wake of the 1969 Stonewall riots in New York City (Duberman, 1994), gay and lesbian activists, believing psychiatric theories to be a major contributor to antihomosexual social stigma, **disrupted** the 1970 and 1971 annual meetings of the APA...

The **protests** were successful in getting organized psychiatry's attention and led to unprecedented and groundbreaking educational panels at the next two annual APA meetings. A 1971 panel, entitled "**Gay is Good**," featured **gay activists** Frank Kameny and Barbara Gittings explaining to psychiatrists, many who were hearing this or the first time, the **stigma** caused by the "homosexuality" diagnosis (Gittings, 2008; Kameny, 2009; Silverstein, 2009).

Kameny and Gittings returned to speak at the 1972 meeting, this time joined by John Fryer, M.D. Fryer appeared as Dr. H Anonymous, a "homosexual psychiatrist" who, given the realistic fear of adverse professional consequences for coming out at that time, disguised his true identity from the audience and spoke of the **discrimination** gay psychiatrists faced in their own profession (Gittings, 2008; Scasta, 2002).

Note that *gay activism* is not merely claimed to be a *catalyst for diagnostic change* but is "the" and "most significant" one. Moreover, the activists disrupted meetings

not due to possession of contrary scientific data but due to their *belief* that psychiatric theories resulted in *antihomosexual social stigma*.
The result of socio-political-moral, and not scientific, based protests was a moral proclamation that "Gay is Good."

The APA published a statement noting:
> ...If homosexuality per se does not meet the criteria for a psychiatric disorder, what is it? Descriptively, it is one form of sexual behavior. Our profession need not now agree on its origin, significance, and value for human happiness when we acknowledge that by itself it does not meet the requirements for a psychiatric disorder. Similarly, by no longer listing it as a psychiatric disorder **we are not saying that it is "normal" or as valuable as heterosexuality**....
>
> What will be the effect of carrying out such a proposal? No doubt, homosexual activist groups will claim that psychiatry has at last recognized that homosexuality is as "normal" as heterosexuality. **They will be wrong**. In removing homosexuality per se from the nomenclature we are only recognizing that by itself homosexuality does not meet the criteria for being considered a psychiatric disorder.
>
> We will in no way be aligning ourselves with any particular viewpoint regarding the etiology or desirability of homosexual behavior (American Psychiatric Association, 1973, pp. 2–3).

Nor did the diagnostic change immediately end psychiatry's pathologizing of some presentations of homosexuality. For in "homosexuality's" place, the DSM-II contained a new diagnosis: Sexual Orientation Disturbance (SOD)...In 1980, DSM-III dropped SOD and in its place substituted "Ego Dystonic Homosexuality" (EDH) (Spitzer, 1981).

Drescher also noted:
...it was obvious to psychiatrists more than a decade later that the inclusion first of SOD, and later EDH, had been **the result of earlier political compromises** and that neither diagnosis met the definition of a disorder in the new nosology (Mass, 1990a, 1990b)...ego-dystonic [basically, a reference to esteem] homosexuality was removed from the next revision, DSM-III-R, in 1987 (Krajeski, 1996)...

In 1992, the World Health Organization (WHO, 1992) removed "homosexuality" from the Tenth Edition of the International Classification of Diseases (ICD-10), replacing it with a diagnosis similar to Ego-Dystonic Homosexuality (Nakajima, 2003).

Currah, Green, and Stryker are quoted to the following effect:
..."**identity politics**," the struggle to articulate new categories of **socially viable** personhood, remains **central** to the consideration of individual rights in the United States, and to the pursuit of a **more**

just social order. **The emergence of "transgender" falls squarely into the identity politics tradition** (p. 3).

Furthermore:
> ...**changing cultural attitudes** about what exactly constitutes "appropriate" expressions of gender are leading some clinicians to encourage parents in **helping their children transition at earlier ages** (Kennedy, 2008; Rosin, 2008; Spiegel, 2008a, 2008b)...as in the case of homosexuality in the 1970s, LGBT **advocacy groups** have had some recent successes in **changing professional opinions** about GID diagnoses.
>
> For example, in November 2008, "After repeated contacts" from the Swedish Association for Sexuality Education (RFSU) and the Swedish Federation for Lesbian, Gay, Bisexual and Transgender Rights (RFSL), the Swedish National Board of Health and Welfare (Transvestitism no longer, 2008), a governmental agency made Sweden the first country to remove the GIDC diagnosis from the Swedish version of the ICD-10, citing its potential, along with five other diagnoses, of being **offensive** and **contributing to prejudice...trans activists**, with the support of LGB and straight allies, are calling for removal of the GID diagnoses. In many respects, these calls resemble historic arguments that led to the 1973 removal of homosexuality from the DSM-II...removing the GID diagnoses from

> DSM could accelerate trans **social acceptance** and **tolerance**.

With reference to the "increasingly militant homophile movement" (homophile being advocacy for homosexuality) Drescher mentions 1969 AD when "the 'homophile movement' evolved into 'gay liberation' and repudiated the medical model of homosexuality. The rest, as they say, is history."

> By the 1950s and 1960s, ambivalence toward the medical model would play out in the publications of the American homophile movement as its members and allies openly debated the relative social merits and costs of pathologizing homosexuality.

At the term "American homophile movement," Drescher's footnotes thusly, "The most notable organizations in this movement were the Mattachine Society for men and the Daughters of Bilitis for women. The Mattachine Review and DOB's The Ladder would publish numerous articles debating normalizing versus pathologizing models."

Thus, you will note the change from militancy and advocacy into the concept of liberation which denotes seeking freedom, rights whilst inciting empathy even from people outside of the in-group and, of course, American's love the underdog.

In this regard, Dr. Margaret Nichols is quoted thusly:
> Ironically, psychiatric diagnosis has also served a humanistic purpose, sometimes for the same groups that it oppresses. Psychiatric classification can initially increase public empathy for people who are

> seen as suffering from a "disease" and can even enable oppressed groups to be treated more humanely, but classification comes at the cost of reinforcing the belief that certain behaviors are deviant, subnormal, or pathological, and therefore less deserving of genuinely equal rights…These events are the result of **changing cultural norms** and they have had a significant impact in rapidly **changing cultural views** on "appropriate" expressions of gender as well.

This ends the specific consideration of homosexual socio-political psychiatric activism but Drescher has a lot more to say on related topics. Thus, we will continue this series within the next segment, "History of sex change reassignment and religious homosexual issue."

Dreschel's Table 1: "lists some of the parallels between homosexuality and gender variance as they relate to psychiatric diagnosis. Homosexuality and GID: Contrasts Possibly Harmful Consequences of Removing GID."

Dreschel's Table 2: "lists some of the contrasts between homosexuality and gender variance as they relate to psychiatric diagnosis. Are Clinical Interventions with Gender Variant Children Reparative Therapy?"

Here is a little info on the history of sex change operations/sex reassignment surgery:
> By the 1920s, physicians in Europe had begun experimenting with sex reassignment surgery (SRS)…1952 New York Daily News headline: "Ex-GI Becomes Blonde Beauty"…For those who eventually would come to identify as transsexual, increased

public discussions of sex reassignment and gender identity would provide them with a way to put a **name** to their **feelings and desires**. As a result, a presentation of gender (Stoller, 1985) once considered exceedingly rare **would gradually become more commonplace**.

Many physicians and psychiatrists criticized using surgery and hormones to irreversibly—and in their view incorrectly—treat people suffering from what they perceived to be either a severe neurotic or psychotic, delusional condition in need of psychotherapy and "reality testing."

With reference to Iran, Drescher notes that "While homosexuality is illegal there, it is estimated that about 150,000 transsexuals live in Iran, which hosts more sex-reassignment surgery (SRS) than any nation besides Thailand." He then references Jesse Ellison's February 19, 2008 AD Newsweek article, "Film Explores Iran's Transsexuals":

Explaining the apparent paradox, one Muslim cleric says that while homosexuality is explicitly outlawed in the Qur'an, sex-change operations are not. They are no more an affront to God's will than, for example, turning wheat into flour and flour into bread. So while homosexuality is punishable by death, sex-change operations are presented as an acceptable alternative—as a way to live within a set of strict gender binaries, as a way to, well, live like others.

The tragic aspect comes through in discussions with patients and their reluctant parents in the waiting room of Tehran's pre-eminent sex-change surgeon, Dr. Bahram Mir Jalali, where it becomes clear that some feel pressured, not free, to become transsexuals. Asked if he would be preparing for surgery were he living outside Iran, one young man says, "No. I wouldn't do it. I wouldn't touch God's work."

Drescher also wrote:
> Rigid gender beliefs often flourish in fundamentalist, religious communities...biblical prohibitions against homosexuality are, at times, framed in language that describes men as transgressing their "natural" (that is, God-given) gender roles...

This last point is interesting because many homosexual activists do not seem to understand that if God is then God is, as the *Declaration of Independence* puts it, "nature's God" and thus, God determines that which is natural as a natural result of His having created it. Homosexual activists, such as Rev. Dr. Mel White (see my book *In Consideration of Rev. Dr. Mel White on Christian Homosexuality*), claim that texts such as "even their women changed the **natural** use into that which is **against nature**. And likewise also the men, leaving the **natural** use of the woman, burned in their lust toward one another; males with males working out shamefulness" (Romans 1) refer to a person's subjective view of themselves; their own desires, orientations, etc. yet, as Drescher rights ups it, "'natural' (that is, God-given)."

He also wrote:
> ...there are...altruistic reasons for turning "sinners" into "patients": the medical model's promise of hope for treatment and cure. An ill person was not necessarily responsible for his or her "symptoms," and,

in the best of circumstances, would benefit
from therapeutic compassion rather than
religious judgment and condemnation...

He also chronicles the following:
In 2005, United Church of Christ became
the first mainline Christian denomination to
support same-sex marriage. Major religious
groups that permit same-sex unions but that
do not give them the same status as marriage
include the Episcopal Church, the
Evangelical Lutheran Church, and Reform
Judaism. Reform Judaism now trains openly
gay and lesbian rabbis...

One wonder if a time comes when idolatry becomes
mainstream hip, trendy and fashionable, the United Church
of Christ, the Episcopal Church, the Evangelical Lutheran
Church, Reform Judaism, et al. will support it and put
clergy-personages in place who will promulgate it.

Drescher notes that "clinicians" Stephen B. Levine and
Anna Solomon wrote:
"Our work **begins** with the belief that GID is
a fact of nature," (p. 51), by which one
might presume they think of transgenderism
as a natural condition, they nevertheless
assert:
1. In a nosological [from *nosology*: the
branch of medical science dealing with the
classification of diseases] sense, GID are
[sic] forms of psychopathology;
2. Gender identity disorders are typically co-
morbid with other psychopathologies;
3. The promotion of civil rights for the
transgendered can obscure professional

perceptions of psychopathology;
4. Ethical obligations require professionals to communicate the uncertainties about the long-term outcome of gender transition and sex reassignment surgery (SRS) [Levine, S. B., & Solomon, A. (2009). Meanings and political implications of "psychopathology" in a gender identity clinic: A report of 10 cases. Journal of Sex & Marital Therapy, 35, p. 41].

Focusing upon the statement that "Our work **begins** with the belief that GID is a fact of nature" note the following:
Moberly (1983a) asserts, "Traditionally, the Christian faith has regarded homosexual activity as inappropriate, as contrary to the will and purposes of God for mankind...it seems to the present writer that one may not avoid the conclusion that homosexual acts are always condemned and never approved. The need for reassessment is not to be found at this point" [Moberly, E. (1983a). Homosexuality: A new Christian ethic. Cambridge, England: James Clarke, p. 27]...

Nicolosi (1991) sees human sexuality through a metaphysical lens that elevates heterosexuality and denigrates same-sex relationships:
Each one of us, man and woman alike, is driven by the power of romantic love. These infatuations gain their power from the unconscious drive to become a complete human being. In heterosexuals, it is the drive to bring together the male-female polarity

> through the longing for the other-than me. But in homosexuals, it is the attempt to fulfill a deficit in wholeness of one's original gender [Nicolosi, J. (1991). Reparative therapy of male homosexuality: A new clinical approach. Northvale, NJ: Aronson, p. 109].
>
> Some significant contrasts between reparative therapists and DSM-V Workgroup members who treat gender variant children are that none of the latter practice from a religious orientation, their published works do not explicitly cite religious dogma, they do not think homosexuality is a sin or an illness, they do not think it is wrong to be gay, they do not see a gay outcome as a treatment failure, they do not call what they do reparative therapy, and they do not reference reparative therapy literature in support of their clinical approaches.

Note that, amongst other issues, Drescher specifies that the "DSM-V Workgroup members" do not "practice from a religious orientation" and "do not explicitly cite religious dogma." However, as evidenced by the example of Levine and Solomon, they do assert secular dogma such as beginning one's research with a presupposition, "Our work **begins** with the belief that GID is a fact of nature." Well, it is a "fact of nature" in as far as it does exist but is it "fact of nature" in that it is natural (as in normal, ethical, beneficial, etc.)?

Moreover, to not "practice from a religious orientation," to "not explicitly cite religious dogma," to "not think homosexuality is a sin or an illness," to "not think it is wrong to be gay," to "not see a gay outcome as a treatment failure," etc. is to be dogmatic. That is to say that they may not cite religious dogma but do cite the secular dogma de jour. Also, note that Drescher makes reference to "religious or other theoretical beliefs."

> ...**generational changes** in the organization, APA gradually became a more **socially conscious** group. Given psychiatry's historical role in stigmatizing homosexuality in mind, and thanks to the efforts of a growing number of **openly gay, lesbian, and bisexual psychiatrists** coming out in the organization (Ashley, 2002; Barber, 2003, 2008; Hire, 2001), APA continued to expand its public positions regarding gay and lesbian civil rights...
>
> In 1998, APA issued a statement opposing "any psychiatric treatment, such as 'reparative' or 'conversion' therapy, that is based on the assumption that homosexuality per se is a mental disorder or is based on the a priori assumption that the patient should change his or her homosexual orientation."
>
> In 2000, APA strengthened the statement, recommending, "ethical practitioners refrain from attempts to change individuals' sexual orientation (American Psychiatric Association, 2000b)"...

The Caucus of Gay, Lesbian, and Bisexual Members of the American Psychiatric Association (CGLBM-APA) was established in the mid 1970s and is active within APA to this day.

In 1978, APA created a task force on gay and lesbian issues that in 1981 was upgraded to a standing Committee on Gay, Lesbian and Bisexual (GLB) Issues. While originally charged to focus on GLB issues, a revised charge was approved and updated in 2004 to include trans issues as well.

Due to a 2009 restructuring of APA governance, the Committee on GLB issues (among scores of others) was "sunsetted" and the GLB Caucus is now the de facto APA component charged with addressing LGBT issues.

Speculative Causes of Homosexuality

Drescher notes:
> ...in the mid-19th century, [Karl Heinrich] Ulrichs (1994) hypothesized that some men were born with a woman's spirit trapped in their bodies. He believed these men constituted a third sex and named them urnings...
>
> Gender beliefs draw upon gender binaries that usually refer to a most ancient one, that of male/female, but can also include the 19th century binary of homosexuality/heterosexuality and, perhaps

in the future, the emerging 21st century
binary of transgender/cisgender.

Cisgender or cissexual refers to "related types of gender identity perceptions, where individuals' experiences of their own gender agree with the sex they were assigned at birth."

> ...mainstream psychiatry and medicine regarded gender incongruent individuals as confused homosexuals, neurotics, transvestites, schizophrenic or some combination thereof (e.g., Socarides, 1969). [Harry] Benjamin..."believed that the transsexual suffers from a biological disorder, that his brain was probably 'feminized' in utero. He eschews any psychological explanation" (Person, 2008, p. 272)...
>
> Robert Stoller...believed that in some cases, childhood family dynamics were responsible for "causing" adult transsexualism...[he held] that GID in boys was a "developmental arrest...in which an excessively close and gratifying mother–infant symbiosis, undisturbed by father's presence, prevents a boy from adequately separating himself from his mother's female body and feminine behavior" (p. 25).

Is Homosexuality a Choice?

Drescher writes:
> APA supports and urges the repeal of all legislation making criminal offenses of

> sexual acts performed by **consenting** adults in **private**....
>
> In 1992, APA called on "all international health organizations, psychiatric organizations, and individual psychiatrists in other countries to urge the repeal in their own countries of legislation that penalizes homosexual acts by **consenting** adults in **private**."

There are a few things to note; firstly the issue of consent makes it clear that the homosexual act and living a homosexual lifestyle are choices. This is because consent is just that, a choice, an agreement. One may have impulses that they did not choose but one still chooses to carry out actions.

Another issue is the concept of privacy as, particularly this year 2015 AD has shown, sexual acts performed by consenting adult homosexuals in private have led to a radical federal level redefinition of marriage for everyone. The same can be said for the social and financial results of sexual acts by consenting adults of any orientation in private when it comes to STDs, abortion, unwanted children, broken families, etc., etc., etc.

Children Issues

Drescher points out:
> In the third edition of the Diagnostic and Statistical Manual of Mental Disorders (DSM-III; APA, 1980), there appeared for the first time two psychiatric diagnoses pertaining to gender dysphoria in children, adolescents, and adults: gender identity

disorder of childhood (GIDC) and transsexualism (the latter was to be used for adolescents and adults).

In the DSM-III-R (APA, 1987), a third diagnosis was added: gender identity disorder of adolescence and adulthood, nontranssexual type. In DSM-IV (APA, 1994, 2000a), this last diagnosis was eliminated ("sunsetted"), and the diagnoses of GIDC and transsexualism were collapsed into one overarching diagnosis, gender identity disorder (GID), with different criteria sets for children versus adolescents and adults. (p. 32)

To Remove or Not to Remove? Insurance is the Question

Drescher writes:
> This diagnosis regarded homosexuality as an illness if an individual with same-sex attractions found them distressing and wanted to change (Spitzer, 1981; Stoller et al., 1973).
>
> The new diagnosis served the purpose of legitimizing the practice of sexual conversion therapies (and presumably justified insurance reimbursement for those interventions as well), even if homosexuality per se was no longer considered an illness. The new diagnosis of SOD also allowed for the unlikely possibility that a person

unhappy about a heterosexual orientation could seek treatment to become gay...

There is no insurance coverage for unofficial problems. The third is that some of the suffering attendant to these patterns can be ameliorated (pp. 43–44)...many health care insurers and other third party payers claim that SRS is an "experimental treatment," an "elective treatment," or "not medically necessary" and therefore not reimbursable...The Swedish diagnostic manual, however, will retain the Transsexualism diagnosis in order to continued providing sex reassignment.

Moreover:
> The closing of [most] U.S. gender clinics created a treatment vacuum which resulted in the slow development of a market economy for the treatment of transsexualism. Free from the restrictive policies of the gender programs, transsexuals began to orchestrate their own sex reassignments...By 1985, there were a number of support groups and regional conferences which welcomed both crossdressers and transsexuals. Around 1990, transsexuals, who had been conspicuously absent from the literature, began to publish, adding their voices to those of feminist scholars...(Denny, 2002, p. 40).

One consequence of less medical control of postoperative living and an increased contact among individuals were newly formed trans communities that proposed a: new [alternative] transgender model, [in which] transsexuals were not mentally ill men and women whose misery could be alleviated only by sex reassignment, but rather [they were] emotionally healthy individuals whose expression of gender was not constrained by societal expectations. Instead, the pathology was shifted from the gender-nonconformist to a society which cannot tolerate difference...

Sexual orientation and transgender identities, once conflated, and only recently separated from each other as discrete categories, now found common political cause. One historical fact supporting such a political alliance was that many of the protestors at the 1969 Stonewall riots were transgender (Duberman, 1994; Stryker, 2007).

Also, with regards to "conflated sexual orientation and gender identity," Drescher states:
Gender identity can be an independent variable in relation to sexual orientation. For example, some people can be born with a male body, have a female gender identity, and, in some cases, be attracted to men (androphilic) while others may be attracted to women (gynephilic).

Same-Sex Marriage
Drescher notes, "Today, polls show a majority of Americans support marriage equality (Langer, 2009)."

Firstly, this is the worst possible argument to be made in favor of same-sex marriage as it leaves its acceptance in the hands of the majority opinion de jour. Thus, if next year, next decade, etc. a majority of Americans oppose, and note how he refers to it, *marriage equality* then what?

Also, changing the traditional definition of marriage came down to one, just one, single person as one, just one, unelected Supreme Court judge's vote changed the definition of "marriage" for the entire nation at the Federal level.

It is noted that the American Psychiatric Association (APA) "issued a 2005 position statement supporting civil marriage equality for gay people."

Appendix: Dr. Kenneth Zucker and "Transgender Kids: Who Knows Best?"

Under consideration is Dr. Kenneth Zucker, the BBC documentary "Transgender Kids: Who Knows Best?," his losing his job and a review of how a medical facility has basically been forced to change its science based methods due to socio-political feelings based activism.

These changes are officially admitted to be based on how "society has also shifted in its understanding and acceptance of gender variance." That medically trained personnel are to "Refrain from treatment of the child that targets reduction of gender-variant behaviors or use of language that pathologises these." And also, how there are such things are "gender-affirming hormones."

I will break up this report so as to cover trans-suicide causes, Dr. Zucker's ousting from academia and the external review of the *Centre for Addiction and Mental Health*. Note that I am not interested in defending Dr. Zucker but am interested in discerning facts from propaganda.

Dr. Zucker is a psychologist and sexologist. He was the Editor-in-Chief of *Archives of Sexual Behavior*. Also, the Psychologist-in-Chief at Toronto's *Centre for Addiction and Mental Health*. And the Head of the *Gender Identity Service*. Plus the Professor in the Departments of Psychiatry and Psychology at the University of Toronto.

Served as Member of the American Psychological Association Task Force on Gender Identity, Gender Variance, and Intersex Conditions. As well as Chair of the American Psychiatric Association workgroup on "Sexual and Gender Identity Disorders" for the 2012 edition of the DSM-5 and had served on workgroups for the DSM-IV and the DSM-IV-TR (*Diagnostic and Statistical Manual of Mental Disorders*).
Additionally, he has many more accolades, credits to his name, etc. for example, he spent more than two decades collating research and clinical data which resulted in his recognition as an international authority on gender identity disorder in children (GIDC) and adolescents.

Discredited by Science or LGBTQIAP+ Activism?

On March 18, 2015 AD Jessica Smith Cross wrote the article, "Outcry prompts CAMH to review its controversial treatment of trans youth," *Metro News* (FYI: CAMH is the *Centre for Addiction and Mental Health*).

So, does life imitate art or does art imitate life? Does the outcry lead to the treatment being considered controversial or does the treatment's being controversial lead to the outcry?
Well, Cross writes that the issue arose "because of outcry from the public" specifically "complaints, particularly from the trans community, that its services 'weren't respectful' of patients' gender identity." Well, supposedly not being "respectful" is not a scientific issue but is an ethical one. This is the tie in with my aforementioned research into the history of the change in views—within the medical as well as societal realms—of LGBTQP about which you can read in the previous appendix.

One issue was that Dr. Zucker's "'conversion therapy' or 'reparative therapy:' [was] designed to stop people from being gay or transgender" as "he believes it is both ethical and possible to direct a young child's gender identity to match their biological sex." Apparently, since this was "a population that already has an increased risk of suicide" then everyone should give in to their feelings and tolerate or accept or approve or not dare voice an opinion. Statements by LGBTQP activists were, for example, that "you cannot change who they are" which is a mere assertion and in fact, there are very many people who not only can change but must change and we all demand that they do so or we lock them up in prisons for decades for various and sundry crimes.

The activism is so very militant that a "bill last week that would ban reparative therapy" and demands were made that "it should be illegal in Ontario" so that now a trained and experienced therapist becomes the criminal. This is even though, "there are two different 'camps' of professional thought on the issue…some believe it works…there are a camp of professionals who do believe in conversion or reparative therapy." Yet, the camp that disagreed with the LGBTQIAP+ commandments de jour should be censored and criminalized is the point being made.

Prior to Cross' article on January 29, 2014 AD, Atana wrote the article, "It's official: Dr. Kenneth Zucker is a criminal in California," *Daily Kos*. Although I should not say that Atana "wrote" it as it is merely a copy and paste job from the activist LGBTQ Nation: I mean *LGBTQ Nation* how militant can you get? Try getting away with establishing an organization called "White Nation" and see how much media and cultural praise you receive.

In any regard, the article(s) notes "a California law that prohibits psychological counseling aimed at changing a minor's sexual orientation." Note the parenthetical editorializing statement in the following direct quotation, "reparative therapy (i.e. torture) for transgender minors, is now a criminal in the state of California" thus, Dr. Kenneth Zucker is a criminal and his therapy is torture but wait, there's more as this was "psychiatric / psychological human rights abuse."

We are told that this is "California's first-in-the nation law barring licensed counselors from offering treatment geared toward changing the sexual orientation of minors." Now, of course, the key is how to define, "sexual orientation" because if sexual orientation is how a person was born then LGBTQIAP+ activists will be the criminals and their getting little kids hooked on hardcore drugs will be seen as torture.
But no, sexual orientation goes back to the issue of feelings: of course, what happens to a little girl who was a *Tomboy* who was manipulated by activist parents to have radically invasive surgery and take years and years' worth of drugs to become a "male" but then realizes later in life that they are just a good ol' fashioned *Tomboy* woman?

The article(s) refers to youngsters who are "being deceived and harmed by unethical therapists who falsely claim they can change a person's sexual orientation." But what of youngsters who are being deceived and harmed by unethical LGBTQP activists who falsely claim they can change a person's sexual nature?

This got so outrageous that wild speculations flew as Jesse Singal noted in his article "A False Accusation Helped Bring Down Kenneth Zucker, a Controversial Sex Researcher," *New York Magazine*, January 27, 2016 AD.

As it turns out an "external review" of CAMH took place which "leveled an array of serious, mostly un-sourced allegations" and "the most incendiary charge concerned Zucker himself: that he had asked an adolescent trans man to take off his shirt, laughed at him, and then called him 'a hairy little vermin,' causing the client great distress" something which the "trans man" later admitted never happened, "CAMH had acknowledged the 'hairy little vermin' accusation was false and had taken down the External Review from its website.
What was the link to the Review now points to a PDF of a 'summary' of that review instead"[25] which I will review next. In fact, note that "there's fairly solid evidence that neither CAMH nor the authors of the review made any effort to verify that [the "trans man"] Adam was actually a patient before posting his claim on the hospital website, leading to its widespread dissemination in news accounts" and that "Neither CAMH administrators nor the review authors responded to questions about the fact-checking process."

CAMH's Public Affairs office told me, "As an employer, CAMH has not issued such a statement" as I asked for "any statements by CAMH as to why Kenneth Zucker is no longer on staff" and they added "Our public statements and media releases are available on our website" and they provided their generic URL.

Therapy Based on Science or LGBTQIAP+ Activism?

Now to CAMH's *Summary of the External Review of the CAMH Gender Identity Clinic of the Child, Youth & Family Services*, January 2016 AD.

Being that which it is, a review, it is generic yet, note that it notes that "a" as in one "community based group" meaning socio-political activists "presented to CAMH a number of concerns" to the effect that "its present practice model was out of step with emerging practices" with "emerging practices" being therapies meant to simply accept and endorse LGBTQP.

The review also notes that "Community stakeholder focus groups were conducted and information was obtained from former patients and family members." I did not realize that science was based on whatever "Community stakeholder focus groups" means—capiche?

Also, "the GIC [Gender Identity Clinic] appears to be" well, I cannot say that "appears to be" is exactly conclusive but hey, this is science so who needs technical accuracy— or right! In any case, they it "appears to be out of step with current clinical and operational practices" based on what? "client and community stakeholder feedback was both positive and negative regarding the clinic" so the common person's opinions varied just as the professional ones do, "Some former clients were very satisfied…others felt the assessment approach was uncomfortable, upsetting and unhelpful." And again, "some" but not all "community stakeholders voiced concerns with regard to the present model of care."

Here is part of the "summary of feedback provided by the reviewers" who were Dr. Suzanne Zinck and Dr. Antonio Pignatiello: FYI: it does not mention Dr. Zucker nor any others by name.[26]

They note:
> Research knowledge and clinical guidelines have evolved, particularly in the last five

> years, and society's understanding and
> acceptance of the diversity of gender
> expression and identity have changed. There
> appears to be a mismatch between literature
> research findings (including those from GIC
> itself), and clinical practice and approach.

Note the emphasis upon who society has changed. The dichotomy mismatch between "literature research findings" and "clinical practice and approach" may mean that the science comes to one conclusion but that which is clinically practiced based on sociopolitical activism comes to another conclusion.
Or, conversely, the neo "literature research findings" are driven by socio-political activism and thus, would demand that scientifically established clinical practices and approached be changed to meet the activism de jour.

At least part of this is described as follows:
> The Clinic describes its approach as a model
> that employs play therapy, cognitive
> behavioural therapy or a combination of
> both as part of its treatment paradigm. Play
> and combination therapy do not reflect
> current approaches to the treatment of
> anxiety, a primary condition of many of the
> clients seen by the GIC and thus this
> practice may be outdated.

So even this noninvasive approach (I mean that play and/or cognitive behavioural therapy is not exactly hardcore drugs or radical surgery) "may be outdated" which means that it may not be.

GIC is viewed by some as being overly-conservative in its patient referral times. A concern was raised with regard to the GIC criteria for diagnosing readiness for referral for gender-affirming hormones and the inherent risk of delays to referral.

This seems to mean that the GIC does not say, "What? Hey, you are a mere child and due to socio-political activism on the part of your parents (or parent, singular, or guardian) you want to radically change your body? Sure, have at it!" Also, note that hardcore pharmaceuticals the specific purpose of which is to radically change that which a person's body is naturally doing are referred to as being "gender-affirming hormones" which is outrageous.

Some of the recommendations by Dr. Zinck and Dr. Pignatiello are as follows.

"Refrain from treatment of the child that targets reduction of gender-variant behaviors or use of language that pathologises these." So, just go with whatever a child demands or, rather, whatever the socio-political activist parents/parent/guardian demands. This is with regards to both aiming at a reduction of behavior and not even employing medically accurate language: this is straight up Orwellian *1984* style "newspeak" censorship. If a child with a perfectly well functioning schmekel wants it sliced to pieces then you cannot imply that there may be something pathologically problematic with that.

Also, "Refrain from allowing parent alone to choose the treatment path" this seems like a balanced failsafe. It would keep either the child or parent from being in full charge of the outcome.

And "Educate parents and children about gender expression, gender identity, gender variance across the lifespan" which is fascinating as that is part of the issue as feelings based gender expression, gender identity and gender variance can and often do in such personages change across the lifespan but what will happen if they have undergone radical reconstructive surgery and turned their bodies into chemistry labs?

Also,
> Refer teens taking hormone-blockers for gender-affirming hormone treatments when ready and eligible in collaboration with endocrinologists involved.

This is just to point out that the teens are taking "hormone-blockers" meaning that their bodies' natural processes are being arrested and radically re-engineered to do something and become something which utterly goes against its own nature—and this is supposed to lead to greater physical and mental health.

The recommendations also move to what I will term turning a medical facility into an activist organization:
> GIC and CAMH as a whole are encouraged to develop a campaign towards collaborative creation of "safe spaces" for transgender children, youth, families, and community caregivers.

Apparently, there will be no "safe spaces" for those who dare to disagree.

The "CAMH's Action Plan" notes that "Knowledge of gender identity and expression has advanced significantly and" note this emphasis, "society has also shifted in its understanding and acceptance of gender variance." Lastly, "At present, the political climate is palpable and this is an emotionally charged issue that would benefit from incorporating all evidence and voices."

Well, the "science" is being changed due to emotion based activism which is utterly unethical but I love honesty and at least their official review is honest enough to admit as much.

"Transgender Kids: Who Knows Best?" Documentary Could Lead to LGBTQP Suicides

Stick with me on this one as it is a wild ride.

The focus upon Dr. Zucker's appearance within John Conroy's BBC documentary *Transgender Kids: Who Knows Best?* Which has brought with it a lot of controversies which I thought to review since much of it is sociopolitical and not scientific.

An example of the outcry comes from Jenny Alto who wrote to the BBC so as to complain:
> It treated adult activists in the transgender community as dangerous meddlers in the treatment of others when in fact they are the survivors of exactly the kind of abuse that doctors like Zucker practice…
>
> This programme was nothing short of an outright attack on a vulnerable and marginalised minority, and in particular on members of that minority who are too young to speak for themselves.
>
> Transgender people have a significantly

> higher incidence of suicide than the general population, and because of attitudes...People kill themselves because of the views the BBC is promoting with programmes like this one.[27]

You may agree, think that this is *too much* or something else yet, this is exactly how the average adult activist in the transgender community reacts: blame other and pepper blame with scare tactics. Subsequently, she wrote to the BBC again to predict, in a manner of speaking, "when the first young trans person has committed suicide because of it what are you going to say to the transgender community then? You can count on it, we won't let you get away."

In other words, when tragically any young trans person commits suicide at any time after the release of the documentary Jenny Alto, et al., will take it upon themselves to blame the BBC, blame Conroy, blame Dr. Zucker, in other words: point fingers all other the place in blame not realizing that when you point one finger at someone there are three fingers pointing back at you.

There are very many factors which go into why there is a shockingly high level of suicide within those who live an LGBTQIAP+ lifestyle and employ LGBTQIAP+ as a worldview. A few examples are that they are literally rebelling against their bodies: they use them in manners in which they were not intended. As their bodies naturally build a certain frame, shape, and brain they take hardcore pharmaceuticals so as to arrest its development. Their nervous system is not able to develop in the manner in which it was meant to. There is also the issue of very many LGBTQIAP+ personages being LGBTQIAP+ due to childhood sexual molestation, etc., etc., etc.

Thus, there is a lot more to it than: documentary + bullying or self-imposed feelings of shame = suicide. I wrote to Alto that "she had referred to "bogus half-truths" and so that she, herself, does not fall into that characterization I pointed out that it is inaccurate make the claim she did regarding suicide.
The research shows that even within countries/cultures wherein such lifestyles are accepted, affirmed, praised, etc. the suicide rates are just as high. For example, "the same dysfunctions exist at inordinately high levels among homosexuals in cultures where the practice is more widely accepted" as per Sandfort, T.G.M.; de Graaf, R.; Bijl, R.V.; Schnabel. Same-sex sexual behavior and psychiatric disorders. Arch. Gen. Psychiatry. 58 (2001): 85-91.

For their part, the BBC replied to Jenny Alto and, in part, noted that Dr. Zucker "believes he was fired for challenging the gender affirmative approach" and that the documentary, "included significant contributions from his critics and supporters of gender affirmation, including transgender activists in Canada and leading medical experts as well as parents with differing experiences of gender dysphoria and gender reassignment."

Having traced the history of how view on LGBTQIAP+ have changed over time are not due to science but due to socio-political activism—along with a general decline in ethics—I recognized certain key terms such as "challenging the gender affirmative approach" meaning just that: daring to disagree with the direction in which the culture was taking itself based on feelings. In fact, that is part of the sharp dichotomy between the science and the activism. It used to be hoped that a "gay gene" or some such thing would be found but this not only never happened but is now viewed as irrelevant.

What matters now? What is the driving force behind the LGBTQIAP+ movement? Feelings, nothing more than feelings. This is why if a non-gender-specific personage feels male today and female tomorrow and both the next day and neither the day after that: all of culture including architecture such as bathrooms are to bend and twist and turn so as to accommodate the fleeting and ever changing feelings de jour.

This is also the point of the documentary: mere children are being placed in the cultural driving seat. Mere children are being told that if they feel a certain way then they are to get on a regimen of hardcore body and mind altering cocktail of drugs which will change them for the rest of their lives—and if anyone disagrees they can lose their jobs, their businesses, their careers, their otherwise good name, be boycotted, etc.

Another symbolic alchemical illustration.

Appendix: Is LGBTQIAP+ Parenting Good for Children?

Technically, that which follows pertains to *homosexual* parenting but as homosexuality touches upon various aspects of the LGBTQIAP+ lifestyles it is relevant all around.

In 2004 AD (with revisions in 2013 AD) Michelle Cretella, MD, FCP, and Den Trumbull, MD, FCP published the paper "Homosexual Parenting: Is It Time For Change?" in via the *American College of Pediatricians* which "is a national medical association of licensed physicians and healthcare professionals who specialize in the care of infants, children, and adolescents. The mission of the College is to enable all children to reach their optimal physical and emotional health and well-being."

One thing that jumped out at me straight away was the qualifying term "asserting" within the abstract:
> Are children reared by two individuals of the same gender as well adjusted as children reared in families with a mother and a father? Until recently the unequivocal answer to this question was "no." Within the last decade, however, professional health organizations,[28] academics, social policymakers and the media have begun asserting that prohibitions on parenting by same-sex couples should be lifted.

In fact, it goes on to specify that these are "far-reaching, generation-changing assertions" and that:
> ...any responsible advocate would rely upon supporting evidence that is comprehensive and conclusive. Not only is this not the situation, but also there is sound evidence that children exposed to the homosexual lifestyle may be at increased risk for emotional, mental, and even physical harm.

If you read the appendix on the history of homosexual socio-political psychiatric activism, you will note that there is a good reason for referring to "generation-changing" as this is an issue wrapped up in socio-political attempts to purposefully change the culture. Also, in some cases such as James Rennie's very many pedophiles are homosexuals and many pedophiles involve themselves in organizations that are meant to advocate for children. Rennie advocated for the homosexual adoption of children only to ensure that pedophiles had legal access to their victims, see my *Pedophiles In High Places* series of articles.[29]

I recall how often during the reality TV show "Wife Swap" poor little children would state that all they want is a mother and a father. Also, a divorced woman was telling me about her child and how he acts like a tough-guy when with his dad but like mommy's little boy when with her: this proves that the child needs a mother and a father or else he would be utterly one sided. As the paper notes, "Clearly, apart from rare situations, depriving a child of one or both biologic parents, **as same-sex parenting requires in every case**, is unhealthy" (emphasis added for emphasis).

The paper notes that more than three decades worth of "of research confirms that children fare best when reared by their two biological parents in a loving low conflict marriage." This helps children "navigate developmental stages," become "more solid in their gender identity" and even "perform better academically, have fewer emotional disorders, and become better functioning adults."[30]

Also, children who grow up in "single parenthood, adoption, and remarriage…face unique challenges.[31] This is due to greater financial challenges, time constraints, spending significantly less time with both biological parents, etc.

I have been calling this and/or the upcoming generations *Generation Emotive Monosyllabic Mouth-Breathing Sociopath* and the paper touches upon aspects of this noting that children who are raised under such circumstances—which are all the hip rage de jour—"experience difficulties forging a relationship" and deal with "divided loyalties." For example, a "baby momma" or "baby daddy" like to see how their temporary sex partner de jour "does with kids" and so kids experience a parade of people who come and go so that the child learns to not build relationships and not develop deep emotions since the evidence before them is that when they do so the next thing they know the person is gone and in comes the next one. Add to this absentee "parents" and divorced parents who do not get along and you have the makings of a sociopath who is most likely to do the same to the next generation.

The paper emphasizes the aforementioned need of a mother and father as in male and female, "There are significant innate differences between male and female that are mediated by genes and hormones and go well beyond basic anatomy." For example, "mothers and fathers parent differently and make unique contributions to the overall development of the child."[32]

It is noted that "mother-love and father-love are qualitatively different."

Now, while "Psychological theory of child development has always recognized the critical role that mothers play in the healthy development of children" poop-culture is socio-politically telling us otherwise based on the concept of *misery loves company* and so attempts are made to make more people like ourselves so as to attempt to alleviate the misery.

You may be aware that Sigmund Freud *far-reachingly and generation-changingly* asserted that religion was an evolutionarily beneficial expression of a human desire for a loving father. Well, he was on to something as Professor of Psychology Paul Vitz turned the tables, researched the lives of the world's most well-known Atheists and determined that in each and every case they had difficulties with their fathers. Either the father was abusive, neglectful, viewed as being weak, was absentee, died while the child was young, etc. Thus, a child's rejection of their earthly lead to a rejection of their Heavenly Father.

See my research of over 133 Atheists wherein I noted just how early in life they became Atheists. It shows that it was not due to science, logic, philosophy, etc. but more based on childish rebellion and childish reasons (and there is a fine line between reason and excuse), see *When and why they became Atheists - Patterns & Statistics*.[33]

The paper notes, "Girls without fathers perform more poorly in school, are more likely to be sexually active and become pregnant as teenagers. Boys without fathers have higher rates of delinquency, violence, and aggression.[34] That is quite the price to pay just so that an extreme minority of our population can have their "PRIDE" and heterosexuals can behave like dogs as Ricardo Montalban once put it, "A great lover is someone who can satisfy one woman her entire lifetime and be satisfied with one woman his entire lifetime. It is not someone who goes from woman to woman; any dog can do that."

It is noted that "Studies that appear to indicate neutral to favorable child outcomes from same-sex parenting have critical design flaws. These include non-longitudinal design, inadequate sample size, biased sample selection, lack of proper controls, failure to account for confounding variables, and perhaps most problematic – all claim to affirm the null hypothesis."[35]

Also:
> Data on the long-term outcomes of children placed in same-sex households is sparse and gives reason for concern.[36]...children reared in same-sex households are more likely to experience sexual confusion, engage in risky sexual experimentation, and later adopt a same-sex identity.[37]...adolescents and young adults who adopt the homosexual lifestyle are at increased risk for mental health problems, including major depression, anxiety disorders, conduct disorders, substance dependence, and especially suicidal ideation and suicide attempts.[38]...children reared by same-sex couples fare worse in a multitude of outcome categories than those reared by heterosexual, married couples.[39]

Other concerns for children in same-sex households is that there are "considerable risks to children exposed to the homosexual lifestyle. Violence between same-sex partners is two to three times more common than among married heterosexual couples."[40]

Moreover, "Same-sex partnerships are significantly more prone to dissolution than heterosexual marriages with the average same-sex relationship lasting only two to three years."[41]
Plus, homosexuals are "promiscuous, with serial sex partners[42]...are more likely...to experience mental illness,[43] substance abuse,[44] suicidal tendencies[45] and shortened life spans."[46]

And in case some would blame homophobia, the paper specifies, "Although some would claim that these dysfunctions are a result of societal pressures in America, the same dysfunctions exist at inordinately high levels among homosexuals in cultures where the practice is more widely accepted."[47]

In a most interesting turn of phrase, the paper concludes by noting that both "tradition and science agree that biological ties and dual gender parenting are protective for children...plays a critical role in forming a secure gender identity, positive emotional well-being, and optimal academic achievement."
This is based on "Decades of social science research" versus "The limited research advocating childrearing by same-sex parents" which "has severe methodological limitations."

Thus, "the American College of Pediatricians believes it is inappropriate, potentially hazardous to children, and dangerously irresponsible to change the age-old prohibition on same-sex parenting, whether by adoption, foster care, or reproductive manipulation. This position is rooted in the best available science."

Appendix: Edgar Cayce, Six-fingered Giants and the Supernatural Creation Gods of Atlantis"

Jim Vieira, stonemason, author, explorer, and host of the *History Channel* shows *Search for the Lost Giants*, wrote an interesting essay titled "Edgar Cayce, Six-fingered Giants and the Supernatural Creation Gods of Atlantis."[48]

This turned into a consideration of the context of this book, which is gender issues, as well as issues pertaining to how the field of research about Nephilim and giants is a cesspool of misinfo and disinfo.

Therein, it is noted that for a styled mystical *reading* which is cited as 364-11, Casey is asked to "give a few details regarding the physiognomy, habits, customs and costumes of the people of Atlantis during the period just before the first destruction," the reply to which is:

> These took on many sizes as to the stature, from that as may be called the midget to the GIANTS – for there were GIANTS IN THE EARTH IN THOSE DAYS, men as tall as (what would be termed today) ten to twelve feet in stature, and well-proportioned throughout.

He is getting the phrase "GIANTS IN THE EARTH IN THOSE DAYS" from Genesis 6:4 and yet, is artificially inserting that this refers to "ten to twelve feet in stature, and well-proportioned throughout."

Since he was reading an English version which employed the vague, generic, subjective and undefined (I can think of 5-6 definitions of *giant*) term giants, he seems to do something typical which is to not define the term contextually but as per whatever popped into his mind du jour—such as fanciful tall tales.

I will leave to the interested reader to consult my 4-6 books (depending on how one counts them) about *giant* related issues.[49]
Behind that text's word *giants* is the word *Nephilim* which does not mean nor does it refer to anything about unusual height. In fact, the Bible never provides us with a reliable physical description of Nephilim so we cannot accept that they were 10-12 ft.

English versions that render (not even translate) *Nephilim* as *giants* are following the Greek Septuagint/LXX version which renders *Nephilim* as *gigantes* yet, this word also does not mean nor does it refer to anything about unusual height but merely and literally means *earth-born*.

Thus, when Vieira follows up with that the Bible is among the texts that "proclaim the existence of ancient giants as well" he is making a very vague statement no matter in which direction one may take it—more to follow.

Edgar Cayce scholar W. H. Church is quoted as having written:
> In what we may term it's primitive or pre-Atlantean phase, before the emergence of its first mighty rulers, in the days of Poseidon and Atlas, or the enlightened reign of Amilius, at what was to become the all-time zenith of Atlantean civilization, the new continent was being busily colonized.

> Already it promised to become what Cayce would call the "Eden of the world", and home to a most unusual race of androgynous soul beings...
> In Hindu mythology, the seed of our present human race were sons of God, who, during the root race associated with the Atlantean epoch, had devolved into semi-divine, androgynous beings, self-imprisoned in bodies, that had physiologically changed, becoming human in appearance.
>
> In this form, they began taking unto themselves wives who were indeed fully human in appearance and fair to gaze upon.[50]

Church is playing upon the play upon Genesis 6 by claiming, "sons of God...associated with the Atlantean epoch" and the rest of it with "self-imprisoned in bodies" stinking of Gnosticism which erroneously view the material/physical realm as being ontologically corrupt. The Genesis 6 allusion is all the more evident with his statement that "they began taking unto themselves wives" as Genesis 6:1-2 and 4 read:

> And it came to pass, when men began to multiply on the face of the earth, and daughters were born unto them, that the sons of God saw the daughters of men that they were fair; and they took them wives of all which they chose...
> There were [Nephilim] in the earth in those days; and also after that, when the sons of God came in unto the daughters of men, and they bare children to them, the same became

mighty men which were of old, men of
renown (King James Version).

Thus, Vieira plays upon the play on the play and notes:
This description is very reminiscent of the
Biblical story of the Nephilim who took on
human wives. Indeed, the Bible clearly
speaks of Giants, six fingers and toes,
androgynous creator gods and a great flood.

The problems with employing terms without defining them continue to cause problems since he makes a very specific statement about "the Biblical story of the Nephilim" but claims, "who took on human wives" which may have been but is not the focus of Genesis 6 which speaks of their dads, the *sons of God*, taking wives and thus, producing Nephilim as their offspring.

He is also very specific about that "the Bible clearly speaks of" but note the plural term "Giants" who thus far has referred to Nephilim, having had "six fingers and toes" but such is simply not the case.

What he has done, without informing his audience and perhaps without realizing it, is to jump context from Nephilim to Rephaim. Sadly, some English version (again, following the LXX) render both of these very different words both as *giants*—and it is generally a terrible idea to render more than one word with just one word; in fact, the LXX also renders *gibborim* as *gigantes*.

Yet, Nephilim are strictly pre-flood hybrids, Rephaim are strictly post-flood mere humans (and there is no relation between them) and gibborim is merely a descriptive term referring to might/mighty.

The issue with "six fingers and toes" is that no such thing is ever stated about Nephilim and Vieira ends up referring to "six fingers and toes, famously associated with the Biblical giant of Gath" but the fact is that such is only stated about one single Repha (Samuel 21:20).

Yet, this was not even "the Biblical giant of Gath" referring to Goliath, but a son of the Biblical giant of Gath, "there was yet a battle in Gath, where was a man of great stature, that had on every hand six fingers, and on every foot six toes, four and twenty in number; and he also was born to the [Repha]"—and note that "great stature" is as subjective as "giant," especially when contextually compared to Israelites, males of which averaged 5.0-5.3 ft. in those days.

As for being "androgynous creator gods" there is no such thing in the entire Bible, although there is "a great flood."

Back to Church, the author that is:
> In the early days of Amilius rule, the separation of the sexes had not yet begun to take place. Though male in their outward aspect, the androgynous sons of God embodied within themselves the nature of both male and female in one person.
>
> By turning to the creative forces, they could become channels to bring into being androgynous progeny after their own kind imbued with a double soul and a double sexed body. In this way, sexual intercourse was unnecessary as a means of propagation.[51]

It is fascinating to note the mental gymnastic machinations Church employs in reviewing Casey: there was no separation of the sexes yet but they were male and since *male* denotes a separation of the sexes he has to claim that in their outward aspect and yet were androgynous and so embodied both sexes' natures.

Vieira notes:
> Many of these creators are described as androgynous like the Egyptian god Khnum. Khnum is depicted on a relief at Esna creating humans on a potter's wheel while the androgynous Thoth writes the years the humans will live behind him.
> Interestingly the Temple of Esna was dedicated to an anonymous androgynous creator god and androgynous Khnum is depicted with six fingers.

Vieira notes the *Israel Exploration Journal*, Volume 57, 2007, wherein Irit Ziffer "explores the idea of androgynous creator deities in his thought-provoking paper, 'The first Adam, Androgyny and the Ain Ghazal two-headed busts.'" He notes that:

> Ziffer explains, "Schmandt-Besserat proposed that the Ain Ghazal statues represented deities, She accounted for the polydactilism (a rare genetic syndrome) of the statues as a divine attribute, and, based on cuneiform literature, identifies the two-headed busts as the likes of the gods Marduk (according to the Epic of Creation, "four were his eyes, four were his ears"; Dalley 1991: 236) and Ishtar ("Ishtar of Nineveh is Tiamat… she has [4 eyes] and 4 ears"; Livingstone 1986: 223; Schmandt-Besserat 1998a: 10–15).
>
> The four eyes and four ears may stand for a doubled face. Barnett WHO (1986: 116; 1986–87; 1990) explained the polydactilism of the ᵃAin Ghazal statues as a mark of

> supernatural entities, such as the biblical Rephaim, a race of giants: "There was a giant of a man, who had six fingers on each hand and six toes on each foot, twenty-four in all; he too was descended from the Rapha (single form of Rephaim). When he taunted Israel, Jonathan, the son of David's brother Shimei, killed him" (2 Sam. 21:20–21).

The term "Rephaim, a race of giants" should biblically read as "Rephaim, a race of Rephaim" but is written to mean "Rephaim, a race of" something of unusual height—yet, again, that unusual height could have been 6 or 6.5 or 7 or 7.5 ft.

Polydactilism is simply a genetic mutation that causes the body to grow extra digits.
Yet, when it comes to divine attribute, extra digits, eyes, heads, arms, legs, and even composite beings (chimeras) seem to not be artistically literally accurate depictions but exaggerations of attributes, as would be becoming of a divinity.
For example, not merely two eyes such as humans have but more—all-seeing, etc.—not two mere arms but more—all doing, etc.—not running on two merely legs but more—swifter, etc.—bigger, stronger, faster, all that and a bag of chips, "Thus, the prototype androgynous human, containing both sexes, was defined through the two-headed person, claims Ziffer."

Vieira writes:
> In Plato's *Symposium* (189-190 AD), Aristophanes displays knowledge of an ancient myth of the androgyne, according to which our original nature was by no means the same as it is now.

> When the androgyne was split into two
> halves, the distinct male and female sexes
> were created.
> Plato is well known for his detailed
> description of Atlantis in the *Timaeus* and
> the *Critias* and the great flood that destroyed
> it but is lesser known for his knowledge of
> ancient androgynous beings...
>
> Philo of Alexandria (the first century AD)
> took up Plato's dualistic conception of the
> creation as well.
>
> Add Berossus, the Midrash, the Gnostics
> and a host of other sources including
> previously mentioned ones to the long list
> who also have.

It seems like Vieira is elephant hurling at this point, he does not quote or cite Philo and there is no such thing as "the Midrash" but there are various Midrashim which span many centuries to boot.
Berossus was a Hellenistic-era Babylonian astronomer, writer, and priest of Bel Marduk—again, no quotations or citations.
The Gnostics refers to just that: the, plural, Gnostics which refers to many different groups—again, no quotations or citations.
And "a host of other sources...the long list" is vague—as the books you are currently reading proves, there is such a long list but my point is about making vague claims.

One such concept I reviewed in this book is mirrored by a statement made by Vieira, "Joannes Richter in his book *The Sky God Dyaeus* makes the remarkable claim that a common global religion which worshipped an androgynous deity existed in deep antiquity" which is, in part, based on that "paleolithic sculptures are quite explicit. Many multi-headed sculptures have been found." Thus, *multi-headed* is interpreted to be literal or indicative of androgyny.

Vieira then focuses on "some of these God-like deities who showed up after the great flood" among whom are:
> Oannes was an androgynous Babylonian man-fish deity…in Mexico, Quetzalcoatl, the demi-god offspring of the androgynous being Ometeotl…The legendary Viracocha, another androgynous god is renowned for his post-flood activities in South America…The Androgynous Thoth is widely reported to have been from Atlantis in esoteric circles, he was also known as Hermes Trismegistus, Hermaphrodite is Hermes + Aphrodite…

Vieira makes an interesting point about how the *Plimpton 322* tablet contains a theorem that predated Pythagoras (570-495 BC) that is "a novel kind of trigonometry based on ratios, not angles and circles…the world's oldest trigonometric table…a base 12 system rather than a base 10 system" about which he asks, "Could this ancient conundrum be easily explained by the fact that these bringers of civilization had six fingers instead of five as has been previously suggested?"

Certainly, why not? Yet, his view is that this has something to do with the paranormal but since extra digits are genetic then it is more readily accessible to propose that such was a family trait of ancient mathematicians in some locale—especially when we consider that ancients were rather fascinated with bodily deformities and may have offered special privileges, such as an education, to a family of some such personages.

Vieira goes on to note the "remarkably specific trait associated with the supernatural ancient ones, six fingers and toes" that "The world is littered with ancient statues, carvings and petroglyphs with six fingers and toes" and that "Even Edgar Cayce reports on a high being with six fingers named Muzuen who traveled to the Gobi Desert from the lost pacific continent of Lemuria in 9,026 BC."

Well, *Lemuria* is actually a term derives from the name of the animal, the lemur, and was literally invented, out of whole cloth in 1864 by zoologist Philip Sclater.
He attempted to elucidate how lemurs ended up in Africa, Madagascar, India, and the islands of the Indian Ocean. He invented the idea of a style continent that would have allowed them to spread abroad.
Yet, some have turned this concept into another Atlantis.

Vieira notes, "The esoteric belief being that six fingers and toes was a trait attributed to ancient supernatural androgynous deities and their offspring…Maybe this is the reason the Biblical Adam is portrayed with six fingers in Jan Van Scorel's painting from 1540." Maybe, but such is all it would be: inspired by esoteric folklore—since there is no reason to think that a painter who lived 1495-1562 AD had any special insights into the reality of how Adam looked.

Finally, note that Vieira wrote, "Hopefully, this information will strike the reader as profoundly as it has me and you will be open to entertain seemingly heretical notions about the past" and while it does strike me profoundly, it does not strike me as he intends but strikes me as rather odd, to say the least, that in this day and age of information overload someone could still provide solid dots of data but connect those dots via vague assertions only and demonstrably erroneous statements.

If when he speaks of such technically simple issues to iron out as the difference between Nephilim and Rephaim and the nature of the term *giants* he misses the mark, it causes me to wonder about his claims about very many ancient cultures and artistic depictions and the various correlations he draws between them into a wonderfully exciting but ultimately questionable narrative.

I propose that similar views amongst cultures who apparently had not connections is actually that after the Tower of Babel event, what was then shared commonly known history came to eventually be called myth and legend as divided humanity took the original history to the *ends of the Earth* and it eventually changed and was augmented on this or that point.

While we are discussing Cayce, I might as well add a few more notes from a few more sources within the overall context of gender issues.

Lynne Rogers wrote the following:
> Hippolytus [170–235 AD], the Greek philosopher, described the Creator as, at once, the "Mind of the Universe, which manages all things, and is male, and a Great Intelligence, which is female and produces all things"…
>
> Most significant of all twin souls mentioned in the [Cayce's] Readings were Jesus and Mary. The Readings state that these two had

many other incarnations, including those as Adam and Eve.

Jessica Madigan, in *Past Lives of Jesus and Mary* (1970), reiterates that the Nubian Hermes, whom Ra Ta met during his exile there, was one of Jesus' previous incarnations...

The earliest of these traditions saw the Goddess as androgynous, both in gender and in the traits often assigned to each gender; thus, the Goddess created the world, nurtured the world and brought death to all beings...

The American Shakers, who believe that God is androgynous, postulate that Jesus as Redeemer is incomplete; the female side of the "redemptive" God has not yet disclosed itself...

The form draws on ideas from previous Goddess tradition sources as well as newer psychological concepts such as scrying, concepts from the Cayce Readings on training the intuition, and other esoteric sources to include the Medicine Wheel, the Kabala and other mystical forms from Eastern and Western traditions. The center fold of the process involves honoring nature, especially the cycles of the moon, the inner self, and one another in the circle as intuitive seeds are planted, developed, and transmuted during corresponding cycles of the waxing, full and waning moon...

A specific Caycean timeline was provided by the *Diamond Lantern* site which reads, in part:
Edgar Cayce's Timeline

12 Million Years Ago:
1st Root Race, first influx of androgynous "ghosts" into Lemuria/MU

10 Million Years Ago:
2nd Root Race, second influx as thought-form projections

310,000 B.C. Atlantean Civilization begins: First truly physical bodies are androgynous "Blue Maze People." 3rd Root Race. First entry into a body. Soul was androgynous so the body was androgynous.

106,000 B.C. FEMALE & MALE Yin & Yang:
The Logos enters to help. Genesis Chapter 2 Yahweh Elohim, Lord God, notices androgynous beings are lonely so he casts a deep sleep upon the Earth and pulls out the feminine side to create two physical beings from the one the feminine and masculine. The Hebrew word Rib and Side are the same word. Hebrew word 'being' and 'man' are the same word. Adam is Eve (i.e. men and women) are equal beings, that together make up the whole being.[52]

Vieira wrote, "Hopefully, this information will strike the reader as profoundly as it has me and you will be open to entertain seemingly heretical notions about the past" and while it does strike me profoundly, it does not strike me as he intends but strikes me as rather odd, to say the least, that in this day and age of information overload someone could still provide solid dots of data but connect those dots via vague assertions only and demonstrably erroneous statements.

The Occult Roots of Postgenderism

Index

A Brief Study Of The Biblical Passages On Gender, 133
A Manifesto For Cyborgs, 124
A Response To Evangelical Feminism, 133
A. B. Holder, 80
Albert Pike, 16
Alexander Strauch, 133
Alison Jaggar, 120, 127
Amaury De Chartres, 10, 21
American College Of Pediatricians, 185, 190
American Psychological Association, 146
American Psychological Association Task Force On Gender Identity, Gender Variance, And Intersex Conditions, 172
Ancient Fragments, 10, 11
Ancient Pagan And Modern Christian Symbolism, 82
Androgynes, 33
Androgynous, 4, 5, 9, 21, 34, 38, 42, 43, 45, 49, 50, 52, 53, 54, 55, 67, 68, 82, 86, 95, 97, 98, 99, 101, 102, 113, 114, 118, 119, 124, 130, 133
Anna Solomon, 160
Ante-Nicene Fathers, 15
Antonio Pignatiello, 176, 178
APA, 145, 146, 148, 152, 153, 163, 164, 165, 166, 170
Archives Of Sexual Behavior, 143, 171
Association For Advancement Of Behavior Therapy, 146
August Bebel, 66
B.Z. Goldberg, 10, 12
Bahram Mir Jalali, 158
Barbara Gittings, 152
Beyond The Gender Binary, 113, 114, 116
Bisexual, 4, 9, 51, 97, 125, 128
Bi-Sexual, 89
Blavatsky, 33, 34, 35, 37, 38, 40, 41, 43, 45, 46, 47, 48, 49, 50, 51, 53, 54, 55, 56, 57, 58, 71, 85
C.A. Musés, 12
CAMH, 172, 175, 179
Caucus Of Gay, Lesbian, And Bisexual Members

Of The American
Psychiatric Association,
164
Cayce, Edgar, 8, 191,
192, 193, 201, 202,
203, 204
Centre For Addiction
And Mental Health,
171, 172
Charlevoix, De Pauw, 79
Charlotte Perkins Gilman,
132
Christian, 139
Christine Jorgensen, 115
Colonel Stanislas Marie
César Famin, 27
Committee On Gay,
Lesbian And Bisexual,
164
Corinthians, 141
Darwin, 53, 54, 55, 56
Darwinian, 36, 53, 54, 71,
129
Daughters Of Bilitis, 156
Den Trumbull, 185
Diagnostic And Statistical
Manual, 143, 166
Diaspora, 119, 128
Divine Pymander, 12
Donald A. Mackenzie, 89
Donna Haraway, 125
Double Sex, 9, 14, 15, 16,
17, 76, 85, 209
Double Sexuality, 67
Double-Sexed, 12, 13, 23,
37, 43, 46, 47, 48, 49,
50, 63, 64, 68, 72, 75,
76, 77, 78, 82, 89, 108
Dr. Phil, 139, 140, 141,
142
DSM, 143, 145, 146, 151,
154, 155, 162, 166
EDH, 154
Edward Carpenter, 9, 79,
86
Ego Dystonic
Homosexuality, 154
Ego-Dystonic
Homosexuality, 154
Ernest Holmes, 95, 96
Ernst Haekel, 72
Esoteric Teachings Of
The Tibetan Tantra, 12
Evolution, 9, 13, 33, 36,
39, 45, 47, 53, 56, 71
Evolutionary, 117, 128,
131
Firmicus, 75, 82
Frank Kameny, 152
Gender Identity
Disorders, 143, 151
Gender Identity Service,
171
Genesis, 5, 22, 36, 44, 49,
67, 69, 86, 97, 98, 99,
100, 101, 102, 114, 209
George Dvorsky, 114
George Foote Moore, 102
George W. Knight III,
134
GID, 143, 151, 155, 157,
160, 161, 162, 165, 167

GIDC, 151, 155, 167
God, 1, 141
Greg Egan, 119, 128
Hargrave Jennings, 10, 19, 21, 106
Hawaiian Creation Chant, 107
Helen Fisher, 129
Herland, 132
Hermaphrodite, 10, 11, 12, 14, 20, 21, 27, 28, 29, 45, 61, 91, 92
Hermaphrodites, 21, 33, 41, 79, 117
Hermaphroditic, 4, 5, 10, 13, 17, 53
Hermaphroditism, 20
Hermaphroditus, 19, 92
Hermes Mercurius Trismegistus, 12
Hermetic Arcanum, 14
History Of Creation, 72
Homosexual, 140
Homosexual Parenting, 185
Homosexuality, 3, 136, 138, 139, 140, 141, 143, 144, 145, 146, 147, 148, 149, 151, 152, 153, 154, 155, 156, 157, 158, 159, 162, 163, 164, 167
Ian Mcdonald, 133
ICD, 154, 155
Intermediate Types Among Primitive Folk, 79
International Classification Of Diseases, 154
Internet Book Of Shadows, 111
Isaac Myer, 105
Isaac P. Cory, 10, 11
Isis Unveiled, 46
Jack Drescher, 143
Jacobus Le Moyne, 79
James Hughes, 114
Jeffrey Eugenides, 133
Jesse Singal, 174
Jessica Smith Cross, 172
Jesus, 1
Joanna Russ, 132
John Conroy, 180, 181
John Fryer, 152
John Godfrey Saxe, 143
John M. Robertson, 75, 82
John Piper, 133
Journal Of Sex & Marital Therapy, 161
Kenneth Zucker, 171, 173, 174, 175
Keri Hulme, 128
Kumulipo, 107, 108
Left Hand Of Darkness, 132
LGBTQ Nation, 173
Lois Mcmaster Bujold, 133

Lost Lemuria, 71
M.D. Fryer, 152
Magus Incognito, 9, 91
Maimonides, 5, 22, 86, 87
Manly P. Hall, 5, 9, 21, 86, 97, 98, 101, 105
Manoel Dias Soeiro, 5, 22
Margaret Nichols, 156
Martha Warren Beckwith, 107
Masculine Cross And Ancient Sex Worship, 23
Matilda Joslyn Gage, 63
Mattachine Society, 156
Mel White, 139, 159
Men And Women, Equal Yet Different, 133
Menasheh Ben Yossef Ben Yisrael, 5, 22
Menasseh Ben Israel, 5, 22
Metamorphoses, 16
Michelle Cretella, 185
Middlesex, 133
Midrash, 5, 102
Morals And Dogma, 16
Moshe Ben Maimon, 5, 22, 87
Motherlines, 132
Myths Of Crete And Pre-Hellenic Europe, 89
National Association Of Social Workers, 146
New Thought, 95

Occult, 4, 9, 40, 45, 53, 97
Ophiolatreia, 10, 59
Ovid, 16
Pagan Christs, 75, 82
Parallels And Contrasts In The History Of Homosexuality, Gender Variance, And The Diagnostic And Statistical Manual, 143
Paul Vitz, 188
Père Lafitau, 81
Peter Singer, 129
Postgender, 3, 4, 53, 113, 114, 117, 125, 128, 133
Postgenderism, 33, 113, 114, 116, 117, 123, 124, 127, 131
Psychiatrists, 141
Psychiatry, 136, 137, 142
Psychologists, 141
Psychology, 114, 136, 137, 140, 142
Queer Diagnoses, 143
Rambam, 22, 87
Ray Kurzweil, 113
Recovering Biblical Manhood And Womanhood, 133
Religious Science, 95, 96
RFSU, 155
River Of Gods, 133
Robert Stoller, 144, 165
Role Relationships Of Men And Women, 134

Rosicrucians, 9, 10, 19, 91, 106
Royal Museum At Naples, 27
Samuel Ben/Bar Nahman/Nahmani, 5, 22, 87
Samuel-Bar-Nachman, 86
Sandra Bem, 130
Science Of Mind, 96
Secret Doctrine Of The Rosicrucians, 9
Secret Teachings Of All Ages, 9, 97, 105
Secret Work Of The Hermetic Philosophy, 14
Sex Change Operation, 113
Sex Reassignment Surgery, 113, 157, 161
Sexual Orientation Disturbance, 154
Sha Rocco, 23
Shulamith Firestone, 122, 123, 126
Sigmund Freud, 145
SOD, 154, 167
Stephen B. Levine, 160
Stonewall Riots, 152, 169
Suzanne Zinck, 176, 178
Suzy Mckee Charnas, 132
Swedish Association For Sexuality Education, 155
Swedish National Board Of Health And Welfare, 155
The Bone People, 128
The Female Man, 132
The Furies, 132
The Miles Vorkosigan, 133
The Qabbalah, 105
The Sacred Fire, 10, 12
The Secret Doctrine, 9, 33, 43, 50, 52, 53, 85, 91
Thousand Nights And A Night, 83
Transgender Kids, 171, 180
Transgenderism, 3, 9, 138
Two-Sexed, 75, 82
Ursula K. Leguin, 132
Vieira, Jim, 191, 192, 194, 195, 196, 197, 198, 199, 200, 201, 204
W. Scott-Elliot, 71
Wayne Grudem, 133
White, 142
Woman, Church And State, 63

Endnotes

[1] See my post "Ancient Aliens' Luciferian Gnosticism": http://www.truefreethinker.com/articles/video-ancient-aliens%e2%80%99-luciferian-gnosticism

[2] Footnotes:

[1] *De Errore Profanarum Religionum*, v. Compare Dionysius the pseudo-Areopagite, Foist. vii *ad Polycarp.*, cited in Selden, *De Diis Syris*, Proleg. c. 3; and in Cudworth, *Intellectual System*, Harrison's ed. i. 482. In a passage in the Yasna there is mention of "the two divine Mithras" (Lenormant, as quoted, citing Burnout). But cp. Mills' rendering of Yasna, i, 11, which appears to be the passage in view.

[2] Sayce, Hibbert Lectures, p. 193.

[3] *Id.* p. 215. Cp. Genesis, i, 27; Donaldson, *Theatre of the Greeks*, 7th ed. p. 21; and Lenormant, *Chaldean Magic*, pp. 129-130. In all likelihood, the Hebrew "Holy Spirit" was originally held to be feminine. Cp. Justin Martyr, 1 Apol. c. 64.

[4] Plutarch, *Isis and Osiris*, c. 43; Seneca, *Quaest. Nat.* iii, 14.

[5] See Servius on the *Æneid*, ii, 632. Cp. Donaldson, as last cited. It was in this way that Apollo and Dionysos came to be at times represented in feminine robes; while Aphroditê was sometimes (as in Sparta) bearded. Cp. Macrobius. *Saturnalia*, iii, 8, as to the double sex of Venus, which is abundantly illustrated by Preller, *Römische Mythologie*, 2nd ed. p. 389, and *Griechische Mythologie*, 2nd ed. i, 268. On other developments of the Principle cp. Selden, *De Diis Syris*, Syntag. ii, c. 2; and Spencer, *De legibus Hebræorum*, lib. ii, c. xvii, § 12. It has been discussed with much suggestiveness, if with some fantasy of speculation, by Mr. Gerald Massey in his *Natural*

Genesis, 1883, i, 510-518.
[6] Anz, *Zur Frage nach dem Ursprung des Gnosticismus*, 1897, p. 105, following Jensen, *Kosmologie der Babylonier*, pp. 142 *sq.*, 272 *sq.*
[7] *Orphica*, ix, 2, 3; x, 18; xliii, 4; lvi, 4.
[8] Cumont, ii, 189-190; i, 235, and *notes*. As we saw, Mithra was also identified with Shamas, the Babylonian Sun-God. *Id.* i, 231.

[3] http://www.truefreethinker.com/articles/religious-science-science-mind-ernest-holmes-part-1-13

[4] June Singer, *Androgyny: Toward a New Theory of Sexuality* (Anchor Books, 1977 AD)

[5] This low resolution image is of a poster for the "The Christine Jorgenson Story" movie and the copyright for it is most likely owned by either the publisher or the creator of the work depicted. It is being used as per fair use in order to illustrate the reference.

[6] http://www.truefreethinker.com/articles/why-do-atheist-countries-lead-production-child-pornography

[7] Dumanoski, Dianne, John Peterson Myers, Theo Colborn. (1997 AD). *Our Stolen Future: Are We Threatening Our Fertility, Intelligence, and Survival?—A Scientific Detective Story*. Plume.

[8] Fukuyama, Francis. (2002 AD). *Our Posthuman Future: Consequences of the Biotechnology Revolution*. New York: Picador.

[9] Brizendine, Louann. (2007). *The Female Brain*. London: Bantam Press. Gender Identity Research and Education Society (GIRES). (2008 AD). *Definition and Synopsis of the Etiology of Adult Gender Identity Disorder and Transsexualism*.

[10] Jaggar, Alison. (1983). *Feminist Politics and Human Nature*. Totowa, N.J: Rowman & Allanheld.

[11] Aldhous, Peter, "Are male eggs and female sperm on the horizon?," New Scientist. February 2, 2008 AD

[12] "Stem cells used to boost breasts," BBC, February 12, 2007 AD

[13] Ludlow, Peter. (1996). *High Noon on the Electronic Frontier: Conceptual Issues In Cyberspace*. Cambridge: MIT Press

[14] Kurzweil, Ray. (2005). *The Singularity is Near: When Humans Transcend Biology*. New York: Viking

[15] University of Adelaide, "Creating Males With Female Sex Chromosomes: Brain Gene Flicks The Switch On Gender," Science Daily, August 20, 2007 AD

[16] Halbert, Debora, "Shulamith Firestone: Radical Feminism and Visions of the Information Society," Information, Communication and Society, 7(1), March: 115-135. (2004 AD)

[17] Sollfrank, Cornelia, "The Truth About Cyberfeminism," 2007 AD

[18] Firestone, Shulamith. (1970 AD). *The Dialectic of Sex*. Bantam Books: N.Y.

[19] Gray, Chris Hables. Ed. (1995 AD). *The Cyborg Handbook*. New York: Routledge.
Plant, Sadie. (1998 AD). *Zeros and Ones: Digital Women + the New Technoculture*. Fourth Estate: London.
Sollfrank, Cornelia, "The Truth About Cyberfeminism," 2007 AD
Wajcman, Judy. (2004 AD). *TechnoFeminism*. Polity Press

[20] Delamater, John D., Janet Shibley Hyde, "Essentialism vs. social constructionism in the study of human sexuality – The Use of Theory in Research and Scholarship on Sexuality," Journal of Sex Research, v35(Feb):10–18. (1998 AD)

[21] Jaggar, Alison. (1983). *Feminist Politics and Human Nature*. Totowa, N.J: Rowman & Allanheld

[22] Barash, David P. and Judith Eve Lipton. (2001 AD). *Myth of Monogamy: Fidelity and Infedility in Animals and People*. W. H. Freeman.

Wilson, Glenn. (1992 AD). *The Great Sex Divide.* Washington D.C.: Scott-Townsend.
[23] Bem, Sandra L., "The measurement of psychological androgyny," J. Consult. Clin. Psychol. 42:155-62. (1974 AD)
Guastello, Denise D. and Stephen J. Guastello, "Androgyny, gender role behavior, and emotional intelligence among college students and their parents," Sex Roles: A Journal of Research, December 2003 AD
[24] Geary, David C., "Male, Female: The Evolution of Sex Differences," American Psychological Association, 2006 AD
[25] http://www.camh.ca/en/hospital/about_camh/newsroom/news_releases_media_advisories_and_backgrounders/current_year/Documents/GIC-Review-26Nov2015.pdf
[26] Dr. Zinck is from Halifax and is in child and adolescent psychiatrist with expertise in gender identity and gender variance, she has practiced for 10 years within a Canadian context. Dr. Pignatiello is a local child and adolescent psychiatrist with 23 years of expertise in systems of care with children and youth presenting with complex needs.
[27] http://jennyalto.blogspot.com/2017/01/bbc-transgender-kids-programme-second.html
[28] American Academy of Pediatrics, "Co-parent or Second-Parent Adoption by Same-Sex Parents," *Pediatrics*. 109(2002 AD): 339-340
[29] http://www.truefreethinker.com/category/pedophilia
[30] Multiple references:
Heuveline, Patrick, et.al. "Shifting Childrearing to Single Mothers: Results from 17 Western Countries," *Population and Development Review*, 29, no.1 (March 2003 AD) p. 48.

Kristen Andersen Moore, et.al., *Marriage from a Child's Perspective: How Does Family Structure Affect Children and What Can We Do About It?* (Washington, D.C.: Child Trends, Research Brief, June 2002 AD) pp.1-2.

Sara McLanahan and Gary Sandfeur, *Growing Up with a Single Parent: What Hurts, What Helps* (Cambridge: Harvard University Press, 1994 AD), p. 45.

Sotirios Sarantakos, "Children in Three Contexts: Family, Education, and Social Development," *Children Australia*, vol. 21 (1996 AD): 23-31.

Jeanne M. Hilton and Esther L. Devall, "Comparison of Parenting and Children's Behavior in Single-Mother, Single-Father, and Intact Families," *Journal of Divorce and Remarriage*, 29 (1998 AD): 23-54.

Elizabeth Thomson et al., "Family Structure and Child Well-Being: Economic Resources vs. Parental Behaviors," *Social Forces*, 73 (1994 AD): 221-42.

David Popenoe, *Life Without Father* (Cambridge: Harvard University Press, 1996 AD), pp. 144, 146.
[31] Multiple references:
Glenn Stanton, *Why Marriage Matters* (Colorado Springs: Pinon Press, 1997 AD) p. 97-153.

SchneiderB, AtteberryA, Owens A. *Family Matters: Family Structure and Child Outcomes*. Birmingham, AL: Alabama Policy Institute; 2005 AD:1-42.Available at http://www.alabamapolicyinstitute.org/PDFs/currentfamily structure.pdf
[32] Multiple references:
Sax, Leonard. *Why Gender Matters: What Parents and Teachers Need to Know About the Emerging Science of Sex Differences* (New York: Doubleday, 2005 AD).

Blankenhorn, David, *Fatherless America*. (New York: Basic books, 1995 AD).

Byrd, Dean. "Gender Complementarity and Child-rearing: Where Tradition and Science Agree," *Journal of Law & Family Studies*, University of Utah, Vol. 6 no. 2, p. 213, 2004 AD.

[33] http://www.truefreethinker.com/articles/when-and-why-they-became-atheists-patterns-statistics

[34] References are to Blankenhorn and Dean

[35] Multiple references:

Robert Lerner, Ph.D., Althea Nagai, Ph.D. *No Basis: What the Studies Don't Tell Us About Same Sex Parenting*, Washington DC; Marriage Law Project/Ethics and Public Policy Center, 2001 AD.

P. Morgan, P. Morgan *Children as Trophies? Examining the Evidence on Same-Sex Parenting*, Newcastle upon Tyne, UK; Christian Institute, 2002 AD.

J. Paul Guiliani and Dwight G. Duncan, "Brief of Amici Curiae Massachusetts Family Institute and National Association for the Research and Therapy of Homosexuality," Appeal to the Supreme Court of Vermont, Docket No. S1009-97CnC.

[36] American Academy of Pediatrics, Perrin, EC, and the committee on psychosocial aspects of child and family health. "Technical report: Co parent or Second-Parent Adoption by Same-Sex Parents," Pediatrics. 109(2002 AD): 343. The Academy acknowledges that the "small, non-representative samples ... and the relatively young age of the children suggest some reserve."

[37] Multiple references:

F. Tasker and S. Golombok, "Adults Raised as Children in

Lesbian Families," *American Journal of Orthopsychiatric Association*, 65 (1995 AD): 213.

J. Michael Bailey et al., "Sexual Orientation of Adult Sons of Gay Fathers," *Developmental Psychology*, 31 (1995 AD): 124-129.

Ibid., pp.127,128.

F. Tasker and S. Golombok, "Do Parents Influence the Sexual Orientation of Their Children?" *Developmental Psychology*, 32 (1996 AD): 7.

Judith Stacey and Timothy J. Biblarz, "(How) Does the Sexual Orientation of Parents Matter," *American Sociological Review*, 66 (2001 AD): 174, 179.

Nanette K. Gartrell, Henny M. W. Bos and Naomi G. Goldberg, "Adolescents of the U.S. National Longitudinal Lesbian Family Study: Sexual Orientation, Sexual Behavior, and Sexual Risk Exposure" *Archive of Sexual Behavior*, 40 (2011 AD):1199-1209, p. 1205.
[38] Stacey and Biblarz
[39] Multiple references:
Mark Regnerus, "How Different are the Adult Children of Parents who have Same-Sex Relationships? Findings from the New Family Structures Study, 41," *Social Science Research*, 752 (2012 AD)

Daniel Potter, "Same-Sex Parent Families and Children's Academic Achievement, 74" *Journal of Marriage & Family*, 556 (2012 AD)
[40] Multiple references:
Gwat Yong Lie and Sabrina Gentlewarrier, "Intimate Violence in Lesbian Relationships: Discussion of Survey

Findings and Practice Implications," *Journal of Social Service Research*, 15 (1991 AD): 41-59.

D. Island and P. Letellier, *Men Who Beat the Men Who Love Them: Battered Gay Men and Domestic Violence* (New York: Haworth Press, 1991 AD), p. 14.

Lettie L. Lockhart et al., "Letting out the Secret: Violence in Lesbian Relationships," *Journal of Interpersonal Violence*, 9 (1994 AD): 469-492.

"Violence Between Intimates," *Bureau of Justice Statistics Selected Findings*, November 1994 AD, p. 2.

Health Implications Associated With Homosexuality (Austin: The Medical Institute for Sexual Health, 1999 AD), p. 79.
[41] Multiple references:
David P. McWhirter and Andrew M. Mattison, *The Male Couple: How Relationships Develop* (Englewood Cliffs: Prentice-Hall, 1984 AD), pp. 252-253.

M. Saghir and E. Robins, *Male and Female Homosexuality* (Baltimore: Williams & Wilkins, 1973), p. 225; L.A. Peplau and H. Amaro, "Understanding Lesbian Relationships," in *Homosexuality: Social, Psychological, and Biological Issues*, ed. J. Weinrich and W. Paul (Beverly Hills: Sage, 1982 AD).

Schumm, Walter R. "Comparative Relationship Stability of Lesbian Mother and Heterosexual Mother Families: A Review of Evidence," *Marriage & Family Review*, 46:8, 2010 AD, 299-509.

M. Pollak, "Male Homosexuality," in *Western Sexuality:*

Practice and Precept in Past and Present Times, ed. P. Aries and A. Bejin, translated by Anthony Forster (New York, NY: B. Blackwell, 1985 AD), pp. 40-61, cited by Joseph Nicolosi in *Reparative Therapy of Male Homosexuality* (Northvale, New Jersey: Jason Aronson Inc., 1991 AD), pp. 124, 125.
[42] Multiple references:
A. P. Bell and M. S. Weinberg, *Homosexualities: A Study of Diversity Among Men and Women* (New York: Simon and Schuster, 1978 AD), pp. 308, 309; See also A. P. Bell, M. S. Weinberg, and S. K. Hammersmith, *Sexual Preference* (Bloomington: Indiana University Press, 1981 AD).

Paul Van de Ven et al., "A Comparative Demographic and Sexual Profile of Older Homosexually Active Men," *Journal of Sex Research*, 34 (1997 AD): 354.

A. A. Deenen, "Intimacy and Sexuality in Gay Male Couples," *Archives of Sexual Behavior*, 23 (1994 AD): 421-431.

"Sex Survey Results," Genre (October 1996), quoted in "Survey Finds 40 percent of Gay Men Have Had More Than 40 Sex Partners," *Lambda Report*, January 1998 AD, p. 20.

Marie Xiridoui, et al., "The Contribution of Steady and Casual Partnerships to the Incidence of HIV infection among Homosexual Men in Amsterdam," *AIDS*, 17 (2003 AD): 1029-1038. [Note: one of the findings of this recent study is that those classified as being in "steady relationships" reported an average of 8 casual partners a year in addition to their partner (p. 1032)]
[43] Multiple references:

J. Bradford et al., "National Lesbian Health Care Survey: Implications for Mental Health Care," *Journal of Consulting and Clinical Psychology*, 62 (1994 AD): 239, cited in Health Implications Associated with Homosexuality, p. 81.

Theo G. M. Sandfort, et al., "Same-sex Sexual Behavior and Psychiatric Disorders," *Archives of General Psychiatry*, 58 (January 2001 AD): 85-91.

Bailey, J. M. Commentary: Homosexuality and mental illness. Arch. Gen. Psychiatry. 56 (1999 AD): 876-880. Author states, "These studies contain arguably the best published data on the association between homosexuality and psychopathology, and both converge on the same unhappy conclusion: homosexual people are at substantially higher risk for some form of emotional problems; including suicidality, major depression, and anxiety disorder, conduct disorder, and nicotine dependence..."
[44] Joanne Hall, "Lesbians Recovering from Alcoholic Problems: An Ethnographic Study of Health Care Expectations," *Nursing Research*, 43 (1994 AD): 238-244.
[45] Multiple references:
R. Herrell et al., "Sexual Orientation and Suicidality, Co-twin Study in Adult Men," *Archives of General Psychiatry*, 56 (1999 AD): 867-874.

Vickie M. Mays, et al., "Risk of Psychiatric Disorders among Individuals Reporting Same-sex Sexual Partners in the National Comorbidity Survey," *American Journal of Public Health*, vol. 91 (June 2001 AD): 933-939.
[46] Robert S. Hogg et al., "Modeling the Impact of HIV Disease on Mortality in Gay and Bisexual Men," *International Journal of Epidemiology*, 26 (1997 AD): 657.

⁴⁷ Sandfort, T.G.M.; de Graaf, R.; Bijl, R.V.; Schnabel. "Same-sex sexual behavior and psychiatric disorders," *Arch. Gen. Psychiatry*, 58 (2001 AD): 85-91.

⁴⁸ Jim Vieira, "Edgar Cayce, Six-fingered Giants and the Supernatural Creation Gods of Atlantis," *Ancient Origins*, parts 1-2, September 27-28, 2017: https://www.ancient-origins.net/myths-legends/edgar-cayce-six-fingered-giants-and-supernatural-creation-gods-atlantis-part-1-008859 https://www.ancient-origins.net/myths-legends/edgar-cayce-six-fingered-giants-and-supernatural-creation-gods-atlantis-part-2-008860

⁴⁹ The most relevant books are:
What Does the Bible Say About Giants and Nephilim? A Styled Giantology and Nephilology

The Apocryphal Nephilim and Giants: Encountering Sons of God, Nephilim, and Giants in Extra-Biblical Texts

The Scholarly Academic Nephilim and Giants: What do Scholarly Academics Say About Nephilim Giants?

Nephilim and Giants as per Pop-Researchers: A comprehensive consideration of the claims of I.D.E. Thomas, Chuck Missler, Dante Fortson, Derek Gilbert, Brian Godawa, Patrick Heron, Thomas Horn, Ken Johnson, L.A. Marzulli, Josh Peck, CK Quarterman, Steve Quayle, Rob Skiba, Gary Wayne, Jim Wilhelmsen, et al.

On the Genesis 6 Affair's Sons of God: Angels or Not? A survey of early Jewish and Christian commentaries including notes on giants and the Nephilim

In Consideration of the Book(s) of Enoch

⁵⁰ W.H. Church, *Edgar Cayce's Story of the Soul* (ARE

Press), pp. 87-89
[51] Church, p. 90
[52] "Why Twin Flames Matter," *Diamond Lantern*: https://www.diamondlantern.com/twin-flames/what-are-twin-flames

CPSIA information can be obtained
at www.ICGtesting.com
Printed in the USA
BVHW051658270423
663175BV00014B/630